Photography:
What's the Law?

PHOTOGRAPHY
What's the Law?

by
Robert M. Cavallo
and
Stuart Kahan

CROWN PUBLISHERS, INC.   *New York*

Printed in the United States of America

Published simultaneously in Canada by General Publishing Company Limited

Library of Congress Cataloging in Publication Data

Cavallo, Robert M
    Photography: what's the law?

    Includes indexes.
    1.   Photography—Law and legislation—United States.   I.   Kahan, Stuart, joint author.   II.   Title.
KF2042.P45C3   344'.73'097   76-781
ISBN 0-517-52534-8

To photographers everywhere

Acknowledgments

The authors gratefully acknowledge the assistance of the following people: Irene Sawuszczak, David Eisendrath, Jonathan Wrice Schults and Jane S. Kinne (of Photo Researchers, Inc.), Lawrence Fried (of ASMP), Walter Shostal and Joseph D. Barnell (of Shostal Associates, Inc.) and Alfred W. Forsyth (of Design Photographers International, Inc.)

Contents

Introduction

This book does not concern itself with f-stops. Neither is it concerned with any other technical aspects of photography nor with the history of photography. It concerns itself with giving the photographer and the user of photography answers—practical answers to everyday questions like this:

> I am going to Ulan Bator, Mongolia, in July. Do I have to ask someone's permission before I take a picture of someone's Ger?

Or this:

> I also want to use that picture to advertise my employer's homes.

Or:

> I just submitted 14 black-and-white positive prints of dogs and cats. The advertising agency lost them. They say I have the negatives so there are no damages. Are they right?

The answers to these questions apply to both photographer and to the advertising agency which may want to know if it is liable for the loss of those cat and dog pictures.

A book publisher may also be involved. It may have certain reprint rights to those pictures. Does this mean any use it may wish to make of them outside the book field?

What then does this book discuss? A quick look at the Table of Contents will tell you where we're headed. We are primarily concerned with giving you practical and realistic information.

Whether photography warrants all this attention is another primary question at this point. The answer, after you read the next few pages, should be readily apparent.

Photography and the photographer are really in the legal ghetto in the arts. It is probably the last of the art professions to emerge as such, and yet it is one of the most rapidly growing of the professions. How many people do you know who have neither a camera nor the desire to own one?

Last year, photographic sales of just equipment topped the $5 billion mark. Half of that sum was spent by amateur photographers of whom it is estimated that there are well over 50 million.

The United States consumes the most merchandise in the photographic field of any country in the world . . . and that includes Japan. In fact, since 1963 Kodak has sold over 50 million of its Instamatic cameras. That's right—50 million.

Taking this one step further, during the twenty-year period from 1952-1972, the photographic industry's growth was *triple* that of the general economy.

Photography has grown so much that many universities are now offering courses leading to a degree with majors in photography. In 1972, Princeton became the first university to establish a professorship in the history of photography.

Photography has made tremendous strides for both the professional and the amateur. New and better processes reach the market every year: self-developing photographs from Polaroid and the use of laser beams, to mention the most recent.

For you professionals, ponder this: Last year, it is estimated that there were well over 100,000 professional photographers in just the United States and well over 25,000 photographic studios.

Photography is being utilized in areas once never thought of, and it's being utilized more than ever.

For example, picture postcards are bigger than ever and we don't mean the French variety. The United States Post Office estimates it handles close to a billion picture postcards a year.

Greeting card companies are utilizing more and more photography as are poster and calendar companies.

Book markets have also mushroomed. A deal was recently completed with a major book publisher for a picture book covering the Bicentennial, involving a television special. The advance to the photographer amounted to $40,000, and in addition, the photographer has a royalty arrangement.

Television programs, motion pictures, educational filmstrips, all have been using photography as if it were going out of style. In fact, one television special, composed entirely of stills, won an award recently for the best documentary of the year.

And with all these uses, the value of even a single transparency has become significant. Would it come as any surprise to you to know that the damage or loss of an original color transparency can now bring as much as $1,500? This is a fact. It has been adjudicated seven times in the Supreme Court of the State of New York in recent arbitration decisions.

As the use of photography continues to spiral, myriad questions arise demanding answers and, in turn, leading to many more questions.

This book, then, is intended to answer those questions in a direct, no-nonsense way. We will be talking about how a photographer can best protect his work, what is involved in copyrighting it, how to avoid invasion of privacy actions, the keystone tips in advertising, the rights in merely taking the photographs, and more.

Note that the law detailed in these pages is primarily New York and federal law. We recognize, of course, that there are fifty states in this country and possibly fifty different sets of laws. However, it should be kept firmly in mind that overriding any of those laws is the federal law. Where there is no federal ruling on a particular subject and your jurisdiction has no ruling either, then you must look to New York inasmuch as the majority of the law in this field has been created from and comes out of the New York jurisdiction. This book is intended to give a general idea of what current law in certain areas is. All law is built on precedent and where there is no law, well, you just have to create it.

If legal advice is required or when in doubt as to what law applies for your locale, the services of a competent professional should be sought. The facts detailed in this book and the forms included are not presented to tell you what to do but simply to inform you about certain laws, regulations and customs, based on our research and experience.

Now, let's find out what happens to the pictures you the photographer take.

Robert M. Cavallo
Stuart Kahan

August, 1975

Photography:
What's the Law?

Can I Take What I Want?

A wide range of questions involves the subjects a photographer may and may not photograph. Note first that we are not talking about using what he takes. That comes later on.

Right now, suppose you, the photographer, are walking down 42nd Street in New York City. You want to take pictures of everything you see: trees cars, buildings, derelicts, theaters, ladies of the night, men of the day, snack bars, etc.

Can you do it?

Of course you can. Take whatever you want. Ah, generally, that is. We have to add a few qualifications. There are certain restrictions (which we will explain), but understand first that you can take all the pictures you want. Later on we will discuss whether you can use them.

Taking pictures on public streets and highways is not forbidden. This does not mean that you can interfere with traffic or otherwise cast yourself in the role of a public nuisance. In some areas and under some conditions, you are a public nuisance by setting up equipment unless you have obtained a permit from the police department. Most prevalent here are the motion picture and television areas where permits are required for filming on the streets. This is especially true in New York City where there are several sections of the Administrative Code requiring permits for the taking of motion pictures or telecasting or photographing in certain public places. Other sections forbid the setting up of tripods in public parks, as potential hazards.

1

Therefore, local ordinances must be investigated and, where applicable, the proper licenses must be secured.

Neither do you want to be a nuisance to another person. It might get you a poke in the nose as a very prominent freelance photographer recently found out.

For ease of understanding, let's break this section down into three headings: People, Places, Things.

PEOPLE

Much has been made of the poor news photographer. You may remember seeing pictures in your local newspapers of photographers having their cameras smashed and other equipment destroyed. The New York Penal Law once had a section (#244 —Law of 1909) which specifically said that a person who "strikes, beats, or wilfully injures the person or apparatus of any news reporter or news photographer during the time when such reporter or photographer is engaged in the pursuit of his occupation or calling in any public place or gathering" is guilty of assault in the third degree.

That, as you can see, was very broad.

But, that section was later consolidated into other sections (Chapter 40, Title H, Article 120) and now reads: "A person is guilty of assault in the third degree when (1) with intent to cause physical injury to another person, he causes such injury to such person or to a third person; or (2) he recklessly causes physical injury to another person; or (3) with criminal negligence, he causes physical injury to another person by means of a deadly weapon or a dangerous instrument."

Note that the specific reference to the news reporter and the news photographer is omitted.

Recently, a black photojournalist was covering the story of an assemblyman. The politician's bodyguards smashed both the photographer and his equipment. Did the newspaper employing the photographer back him up? No. Why? Because he was black? Because he was a photographer? No reason was given. Apparently, somebody thought the photographer was provoking the poor assemblyman. It is quite obvious that, for whatever reasons, the photographer's vulnerability is becoming more and more apparent. The Constitution, you say, grants freedom of the press? That's true. But, as case law has shown, the constitutional guarantee of free speech and free press was never in-

2

tended as an invitation for fraud or as a license for illegality or immorality.

Cases have now cropped up in which a photographer failed to obey a policeman's command to move from a particular area, thus endangering the public peace. This has been held to amount to disorderly conduct. There is no question that there is a clash between Freedom of Press and Speech and local ordinances.

The key to all this is the words "disorderly conduct to possibly endanger public peace."

In a recent case involving a freelance photographer and the widow of a former president, the court noted that the photographer's business was a lawful one (an understatement to say the least) and, therefore, could not be prohibited, but his *personal* conduct could be regulated and controlled.

The line here is a fine one. And it now becomes a question of who does the regulating and under what circumstances. The new law on third degree assault in New York, as cited above, does not help the photographer, especially coupled with what the courts have been handing down.

What happens then to those pictures you want to take on 42nd Street? Well, you might bear in mind that some people just don't like to have their pictures taken. Even though you can take all the pictures you want (within the guidelines of not being a pest or a menace to traffic, etc.), you might just wind up with a flattened nose if you step out of those vague guidelines—and the law may not be particularly helpful.

Caution, then, is the byword.

PLACES

What about concert halls, theaters, museums, stadiums, hospitals, nursing homes and the like?

For the most part, you can take pictures in such places unless there are clear rules or regulations to the contrary. With respect specifically to museums, you might take note of the fact that the typical United States museum is privately controlled, supervised by its own board of trustees and supported by tax-exempt endowments or gifts. Because of this, those museums are generally not subject to direct state or federal regulations; therefore, in the areas where custom and usage prevail, those museums have developed their own set of rules.

3

If a museum is privately controlled, you must follow the regulations. You may not trespass. If it is public, do what you want as long as you are not creating a hazard or a public nuisance. Naturally, you must be guided by whatever lawful signs you see. One thing you don't need is a citation for trespass.

The courtroom, as most of you are aware, or should be, is a different situation. The taking of photographs in a courtroom at any time, whether or not the court is in session, is prohibited unless permission is first obtained. In New York, this is carefully detailed in the Rules of the Administrative Board of the Judicial Conference of the State of New York. The fact to consider is that everything revolves around the "dignity" of the courtroom.

There was a case where for three days nobody knew that a certain party was taking pictures. A small, nondescript man sat in a corner of the courtroom during a rather sensational trial, with a 35mm camera strapped to his wrist, clicking his false teeth every time the shutter snapped. It took a solid three days before he was discovered and only because the camera (not the teeth) inadvertently dropped to the floor.

There is an inconsistency, however. If artistic sketches can be made of a trial, which are then telecast that very evening, what is the big to-do about a nonclicking, nonflashing camera? Even if cameras were allowed, what is the problem? Would knowledge of pictures being taken change the performances in the courtroom any more than those in Senate or House Judiciary hearings which are televised before the world? Perhaps the courts are worried about publicity or the publication of photographed materials and personages. Perhaps also the answer might be to hold publication of materials until after the trial is complete. But, whatever, something should be done to improve this situation. In the meantime, no cameras without permission.

Much has been said about defense installations. Title 18, United States Code, Section 795-797, says that whenever in the interests of national defense the President of the United States declares that certain vital military and naval installations or equipment shall be privileged, then it is unlawful to take any photographs of such installations or equipment without permission of proper authorities.

This law, admittedly, is quite broad, covering not only the installations but the equipment itself and applies whether the photographs are taken from the ground or from the air.

You must be familiar with this law.

Finally, let's consider one more place: your studio. Are you restricted from doing what you want in the privacy of your studio?

Well, the only restrictions which might apply would be if there were any specific local rules or ordinances. Not too long ago, a number of states had restrictions on what kinds of businesses could be operated on what days. Pennsylvania most notably had the infamous blue laws.

Depending on where your photographic studio sits, there may be a multitude of laws and regulations. Leases by owners of buildings may have certain restrictions. There may be other restrictions imposed by the local authorities, even between countries.

For example, if you set up shop in England, you would be exposed to various regulations concerning not only the use of the studio, but even alterations you may want to make to the premises.

We have even seen a charge levied by town authorities for the right of a photographer to discharge certain chemicals into the town's sewer system. But, returning to our original trend of thought, in the absence of specific regulations there is nothing in the New York statutes (for those residing here) which would restrict your working in your studio whenever you wanted. Those outside New York should check the restrictions, if any, in their area.

The prohibition about taking photographs in concert halls, theaters, and the like is primarily a copyright problem and these areas are discussed in Chapter 5 of this book.

THINGS

You are fairly free to photograph most things, such as cars and trees and manhole covers . . . even garbage. At least, there is no specific law preventing you, at this time, from doing so. Things, then, are generally not a problem, except the photographing of money, postage stamps and securities, which is a highly delicate area as far as the United States Government is concerned. You first must check your sources as to what is required.

The law in this area has been modified, changed, added to and played with at a cost of more than the value of the money it strives to protect.

Originally, under the U.S. law (Title 18, U.S. Code, Section 474), it was a crime to photograph a U.S. treasury note. This included all securities, bonds and currency. In fact, if you went searching for the law, you would find it more easily by looking under the section entitled "Counterfeiting." That's exactly how important it was. We do say "was."

The law has been relaxed somewhat although certain areas are still open to many interpretations and there are still holes wide enough to drive tractors through. Basically, it comes down to this. Under Section 504 of Title 18, United States Code, prints may now be made of U.S. postage stamps, U.S. revenue stamps, any obligation or security of the United States, and postage stamps, revenue stamps, notes, bonds and other obligations or securities of any foreign government, bank or corporation.

However, and watch this carefully: These prints may be used only for philatelic, numismatic, educational, historical or newsworthy purposes such as in articles, books, journals, newspapers, etc., *and* they may not be used for advertising purposes.

Another proviso: The exception to this advertising rule is for illustrations of stamps and paper money in legitimate advertising of legitimate numismatists, stamp dealers, etc.

It gets even more involved. The above regulations are for black-and-white except for illustrations of U.S. or foreign postage stamps, which can be in color.

We haven't even touched the other guidelines, covering sizes of reproductions, distortions, demonetized stamps of foreign countries and the like. This is a large, complex variety of requirements, so that if you must photograph something specific, you had better check the Federal Code, or with your attorney. Motion picture films, microfilms or slides for screen projections and telecasting of the above can be made provided they are done for the purposes outlined above. In these media there doesn't seem to be any restriction as to color or black-and-white.

One other fact. No prints or other reproductions can be made from such motion picture films or slides except for the purposes outlined above and provided you have the permission of the U.S. Secretary of the Treasury.

Flags and seals are another tricky area. Under Title 4 of the United States Code, Chapter 1, Section 3, there is a restriction against any advertising on the "flag, standard, colors or ensign" of the United States. This is applicable to the District of Columbia regarding the use of these items in connection with advertising purposes. The improper use of the national flag outside the District of Columbia has not been made a federal offense but should Congress wish to assume such control, it has the power to do so under the Constitution.

It should be noted that the protection of the national flag against illegitimate uses is not so exclusively entrusted to the federal government as to prevent a state from making it a misdemeanor to use representations of such flag upon articles or merchandise for advertising purposes. Accordingly, a statute in a particular state may forbid the use of the national flag, or even its own state flag, for certain purposes. Therefore it would be best to check the statutes in your particular state as to what prohibition exists on photographing the national or state flag and the national or state seal. Otherwise, have fun!

TO SUMMARIZE

Subject to certain restrictions and certain guidelines, in most instances, you can take what you want, but remember:
1. *Do not trespass.*
2. *As to courtrooms, museums, etc., understand that the law has rigid standards.*
3. *As to money, stamps, securities, flags, seals, there are different guidelines to be followed.*

Use, of course, is another matter, but before we come to that, we must first find out whether you own what you take.

Do I Own What I Take?

It is the question of ownership of the products of his labor that seems to surprise the photographer more than any other. As a matter of fact, it doesn't just surprise him; it shocks him.

This stems primarily from the fact that the photographer is, by and large, ignorant of the law in this regard. If he really knew what the law said, he would spend countless sleepless nights.

Let's make one sweeping statement of fact: In absence of an agreement to the contrary, the employer, sitter, boss, client, customer owns everything. Shocking? But true.

Now, let's find out where this statement originates and what the photographer can do to protect himself. The starting point dates back to 1913. Although there were many cases dealing with ownership of materials before 1913, it wasn't until then that the real "General Rule of Law" was established.

The case took place in New York (as the majority of the landmark decisions in this area do) and it is the bedrock of the law which still exists today.

In the case of *White Studio, Inc.* v. *Dreyfoos* (156 AD 762) White claimed that Dreyfoos took a work originally photographed by White and reproduced it without White's permission, even though the original sitter for the photograph had granted permission to Dreyfoos.

The court decided that the ordering contract between a photographer and his customers was a contract of employment.

Therefore, the conception as well as the production of the photograph was work done for the customers and they, not their employees (the photographers), were the exclusive owners of all proprietary rights.

Read that again. "They," not their employees (the photographers), were the exclusive owners of all proprietary rights. Who then is the customer? The party originally sitting for the photograph. Who is the employee? Why, White, of course.

The court then set down what is known today as the "General Rule of Law"; to wit, the ordinary contract between a photographer and his customer is one of employment. The customer, as employer, is exclusive owner of all proprietary rights, both in the conception and the production of the work. With this General Rule of Law firmly in mind, many side issues arose requiring the court's determination. One such side issue was "custom and usage."

In 1946, the court ruled that custom and usage could not be set up to oppose or alter a general principle or rule of law in order to make the legal rights or liabilities of the parties other than they are under the common law (meaning the old English law upon which most of our law is based) or as fixed by the circumstances of the transaction (*Colten* v. *Jacques Marchais, Inc.*, 61 NYS 2d 269).

This decision came about when a commercial photographer sought to plead certain custom and usage in the field of commercial photography to a lawsuit. He claimed that custom and usage gave him a right to own and possess the negatives of photographs made for his customer.

The White case concerned itself with portrait photographers. But, with the 1946 decision and a Federal decision ten years later, the court once and for all handled the question of all photographers—commercial and portrait alike.

In 1956, came the matter of *Avedon* v. *Exstein* et al (141 F. Supp. 278).

Richard Avedon, a famous commercial photographer, brought suit against a number of companies: Marboro Books, Cowles magazines, Curtis Publishing, The New York Times, to name but a few, in addition to Exstein, an advertising agency. The suit involved infringement of copyright and breach of contract.

Avedon was retained by Exstein to make a photograph of a specific subject to be used in an advertisement to be placed in *The New York Times*. Exstein was the advertising agency requesting the work. Avedon took the photograph, delivered it and was paid for it. The photograph appeared, as planned, in *The New York Times.*

Subsequently, Avedon also delivered the negative to one of the defendants. Thereafter, Exstein sold the photograph to another of the defendants who used it with some minor retouching to advertise a number of magazines.

Avedon claimed that in dealings between commercial photographers and advertising agencies, custom and usage would and should prevail and, therefore, he would be the owner of the negative.

The defendants, on the other hand, contended that evidence of custom and usage could not be offered to alter a general rule of law and that there was such a general rule of law to the effect that a photographer who was employed to take a picture for a client retained no rights in the picture after delivery, except as are expressly reserved.

Avedon was not stopped. He conceded that yes indeed there was a long line of photography cases holding that all rights to a picture belong to the client who hired the photographer. Furthermore, he even admitted that if this rule of law were applicable, he would not be able to offer evidence of custom and usage. But, to avoid this, Avedon argued instead that such a rule of law was applicable only to portrait photographers. He said that the purpose of the rule in portrait photography cases was to prevent a "breach of confidence" whereby a photographer could "cause mischief to the unwary person who did not realize that his portrait might be susceptible to . . . future uses." This protection, Avedon claimed, is not needed in commercial photography.

The court did not agree. It didn't feel there was any less need for this kind of protection in commercial photography than in portrait photography. Relying on cases where prior courts had stated that usage and custom could not be set up to oppose or alter a general principle or rule of law and make the legal rights or liabilities of the parties other than they are by the common law or as fixed by the circumstances of the transaction, this court said that since Avedon could not offer evidence of custom and usage, his allegations must fail.

In effect then, the court held that the relationship between a commercial photographer and an advertising agency is no different from that between a portrait photographer and his customer, and that custom and usage would not be permitted to alter this rule.

The courts today generally follow the rule: when a photographer receives an assignment from, say, a magazine, to take certain photographs for a fee, the photographs will be *owned by the magazine*, as long as there is no agreement to the contrary. However, watch those last ten words. We'll be coming back to them time and time again.

Another side issue. Who owns the negative?

In one case, the court ruled that there was nothing inconsistent with the proprietary rights belonging to the customer and custody of the plates remaining with the photographer.

When a person engages a photographer to take his picture, agreeing to pay so much for the copies which he desires, the transaction assumes the form of a contract and it is a breach of contract, as well as a violation of confidence, for the photographer to make additional copies from the negative. The negative may belong to the photographer but the right to print additional copies is the right of the customer. (*Corliss v. E. W. Walker Co.*, 64 F 280)

So, what is the photographer?

The photographer has now become a warehouse for the customer. Why be a warehouse when you could be an owner. How? Remember those ten words? If the photographer will learn to enter into agreements whenever he works for somebody, he will not wind up on the short end of the ownership stick.

Does this mean the photographer needs a battery of lawyers on each session or assignment? No. Sample forms of how a photographer can protect himself are included in Chapter 8.

But what happens when a third party arranges for a photograph? Suppose someone comes to you via another party. Who owns what? Let's go to a case known as *Lumiere* v. *Robertson-Cole Distributing Corporation* (280 F. 550 [1922]).

Lumiere is a photographer. Robertson-Cole is a producer of motion pictures. Robertson-Cole employs a chap named Carpentier, a fighter, to appear as an actor in motion pictures and a fellow named Adolfi to direct the motion pictures. Lumiere, by the way, has an agent named Letendre.

Now, Robertson-Cole wants photographs taken of Carpentier for the purpose of advertising the motion pictures. Letendre and Adolfi enter into an arrangement for the taking of such photographs. Adolfi advises that Robertson-Cole is paying for them.

An appointment is made with Lumiere to bring Carpentier to the studio for sittings. Carpentier is accompanied by his manager and an interpreter. (Only one of the three speaks English). Letendre, thinking quickly (as most agents do) wants Carpentier to sign a letter agreement giving his boss Lumiere copyright in the photographs to be taken. Letendre submits the letter agreement to Adolfi inasmuch as he considers him the one in charge of the operation. The letter isn't signed.

The photographs are taken, the finished prints are sent to Robertson-Cole and Robertson-Cole pays for them. In the meantime, Lumiere and Letendre prepare another letter agreement for Carpentier to sign and such agreement is signed to the effect that Lumiere has the copyright to the photographs.

Of course, the question arises as to whether the non-English-speaking Carpentier and his non-English-speaking manager knew the contents or effect of the letter that was thrust in front of them. (Apparently, the interpreter was in the coffee shop at the time.) But, we don't bother with that. Here comes the lawsuit!

The question is who owns what?

The trial is a masterful display of confusion. Claims and counterclaims, statements and cross-statements fly around the courtroom. What Lumiere wants is that Robertson-Cole be restrained by injunction from offering for sale or otherwise distributing copies of the photographs of Carpentier and that he (Lumiere) also be awarded damages suffered for alleged wrongful publication.

What does the court find?

First, it reiterates what we have explained before. The usual contract between a photographer and his customer is one of employment. The production of the photograph is work done for the customer, not for the photographer, and the sitter is entitled to all proprietary rights therein. Neither the artist nor anyone else has any right to make pictures from the negative or to copy the photographs, if not otherwise published, for anyone else. The *sitter* is entitled to all rights?

The court narrows the matter.

Where a photographer, it says, takes photographs of a person who goes or is sent to the photographer in the usual course, and the photographer is paid for the photographs and for his services in taking the photographs, the right of copyright is in the sitter *or in the person sending the sitter to be photographed* and it is not in the photographer. (The emphasis is ours).

Therefore, said the court, the pictures of Carpentier were taken at the instance of Robertson-Cole, and Lumiere was paid by Robertson-Cole, and accordingly, the right to copyright resided in Robertson-Cole.

So, what does it come down to? Well, the fact is that the fighter was not the customer. He was simply the object of the photography.

With this under our belt, let's go further. What happens with copies that are made of photographs? Who owns them?

> The authorities are generally agreed that in the absence of special or peculiar circumstances, a photographer who is employed to make a photograph for another has no right, without express authorization, to make copies thereof from the negative for his own use or profit, the decisions being generally based upon the theory of an implied contractual restriction, although some cases have asserted the additional ground of violation of confidence, right of privacy and right of property. (58 *American Jurisprudence* 2d, 76)

Let's check this out. An interesting case arose in 1942 concerning Ylla, a well-known photographer of animals (*Lawrence v. Ylla*, 184 Misc. N.Y., 807).

In June of that year, Ruth Lawrence requested that one Yela Koffler (known as "Ylla") take photographs of her dog. What eventually evolved is one of the more famous and noteworthy cases in the annals of photography. The only agreement entered into between the parties was with respect to the price of the photographs.

Ylla made three dozen pictures of the dog and thereafter sent Lawrence prints of the best of those pictures for selection. Lawrence made a selection and paid Koffler for two positive prints. Subsequently, she made a further payment for two more prints. One of the defendants, Rapho-Guillemette Pictures, was acting as agent for Ylla. That company thereafter submitted to McCann-Erickson, an advertising agency, a number of pictures of dogs which Ylla had taken, among them the picture of Lawrence's dog. McCann-Erickson purchased the positive print of Lawrence's dog, acting as agents for the National Biscuit

Company. They paid the sum of $25. Beginning in February of 1943, the National Biscuit Company caused to be inserted in five separate newspapers various ads which included the picture of the Lawrence dog. *The New York Times* and the *Daily News* each published the ad on several occasions.

It is worth noting that the evidence did not disclose that Mc-Cann-Erickson, National Biscuit, the *Times* and the *News* were ever aware of Lawrence's existence or of any of her rights to the negative or the photograph in controversy. Thus, Lawrence failed to establish that there was either a fiduciary relationship (meaning a relationship based on confidence and trust) or any privity of contract (that is, a connection) with those four defendants. Accordingly, claim to damages would have to be asserted solely against Ylla and Rapho-Guillemette, the agent.

Lawrence's property right stemmed directly and exclusively from her contract with the photographer Ylla, by which the photographer's agent was also bound. In other words, whatever rights a person may have in a photograph are dependent upon the existence of a contractual relationship between that person and the photographer. If, for example, a photograph of a dog happens to be taken by a photographer on his own initiative, without any arrangement with the owner of the dog for payment, all property interest in the photograph, including the right to copyright the same, lies solely with the photographer. That's called a gratuitous photograph and is discussed shortly.

In the Ylla case, the court ruled that Lawrence was entitled to a permanent injunction against all of the defendants, restraining any further use of the dog's photograph but that so far as an accounting was concerned, she was entitled to relief only against Ylla and the agent and, accordingly, she would have costs against those two. All right, let's sum it all up. At this point, what do we know? Well, first we know that as and between a photographer and a person who sits for a photographer, the proprietary rights to the photograph belong to the customer, and the photographer may not make or distribute copies without the customer's consent. Secondly, we know that in the absence of an agreement to the contrary, the photographer may, however, retain custody of the negatives in accordance with trade custom, although he may not use them without the customer's permission.

But, we cannot leave this ownership question as yet. We have a few elements dangling: What about the copyrighted photograph? What about the gratuitous photograph? And what about the implied contract? The first of the side issues is the gratuitous photograph. What do we mean by a gratuitous photograph? Simply, it is a photograph taken by a photographer for *his* own benefit. Accordingly, he is entitled to the copyright. In other words, where the photograph is taken at the expense of the photographer and for his benefit, the sitter loses control of the disposition of the photographs and the property right rests with the photographer.

Is this the only way a photographer can get the copyright in what he takes? No. He can get it by agreement, either with the sitter or with the sitter's agent. Watch those agents. In this regard, let's take another case of our friend Lumiere. (*Lumiere* v. *Pathe-Exchange, Inc.*, 275 F. 428 [1921])

In May, 1918, a motion picture actress named Dolores Cassinelli employed Letendre as her publicity agent. Naturally, being the good agent he is, Letendre told Miss Cassinelli that it would be necessary for her to have artistic photographs taken to be used for publicity purposes. Guess whom he suggested as the photographer?

In June, 1918, she ordered and paid for some two hundred photographs. The proofs given Miss Cassinelli were all marked as copyrighted by Lumiere. How did they get that way? Miss Cassinelli left the business decisions in the hands of Letendre and he agreed with Lumiere that the latter would have the copyright.

At the trial, Miss Cassinelli testified that she didn't remember agreeing to that but she had referred the entire matter of business to Letendre, concerning herself solely with the artistic details and values.

The court, after hearing all the testimony, said:

> Although it is perfectly evident that she did not know anything about copyright or what it meant, the evidence satisfies us that Letendre acted within his authority as her agent in giving the copyright privilege to the plaintiff.

Who has what rights to a copyright can be determined by the law, by an agreement or by a certain set of facts.

Let's suppose you the photographer have been called by a committee of the graduating class of 1976, at your local high school, to take the class picture. The class has already arranged with a local printing company to print its class yearbook which is to contain the group photograph of the class, the one you are going to take. Now, as part of the agreement, you agree with the class that there is to be no fee paid to you for your services but for each photograph which a class member wants, you will charge $4.50. Fair enough.

So, on a bright sunny day toward the end of May, you assemble the 999 class members on the front steps of the high school. You group them, arrange their positions and do whatever else is necessary to secure a proper negative from which good prints can be made. After all, 999 members times four and a half. . . .

The negative comes out so well that you decide to register your work in the copyright office. This you do and you receive back a certificate of registration from the U.S. Copyright Office. You give a proof of your work (with a copyright legend in the corner) to the class committee and you wait for the orders to roll in.

Let's see. Each member will obviously want at least one for himself, one for the parents, one for the grandparents and one for the girl friend who lives down the lane. All times $4.50.

While you are filling out your bank deposit slip, the printing company tells the class committee that the photograph is too large. They will have to cut it down considerably. In fact, by the time they are done, only the members of the class are left, with a scant margin around the four sides. The trees, steps, sky, high school building *and* the copyright legend are all gone.

Well, in this reduced condition, the photograph is eventually taken by the class committee to an engraving company which makes a copper cut from it. A decision is made that instead of including the picture as part of the class book, it will be printed separately and distributed to each member of the class along with the yearbook.

You find out.

There is no question what you do. It's a suit against everybody for copyright infringement.

Nothing bothers the defendants though. Their defense is simple. The sitter owns everything. Thus, the property right in this photograph belongs to the high school class. Okay, now, if you were the judge, what do you say? Well, no, said the court. That isn't exactly the way we see it.

The defense would be true if the committee and the photographer had entered into a contract whereby the committee was to pay the photographer a fixed price for his services. But, that's not the case. The photographer was only to take the group picture and charge each individual who wished to make a purchase, $4.50 per photograph. No other conclusion is possible except one: The photographer was the lawful owner of the rights in the photograph, bound only to sell each photograph at a price not to exceed $4.50 to each member of the class desiring to purchase one.

"By no possible stretch of the evidence could it be said that the class had or owned the right in the photograph."

You will note the quotes around the preceding sentence. This hypothetical case is based on an actual one . . . a landmark decision back in 1916: *Altman* v. *New Haven Union Co.*, 254 F. 113.

The final point to be considered is the implied contract. In 1971, a suit was instituted against a major magazine publisher and a major airline for the loss of some 3250 original color transparencies.

The photographer was a stringer for the publishing company and was in Alaska covering certain projects, among them a study of Alaskan foods for a series of books on famous foods of the world. The photographer completed approximately ten weeks of shooting and turned his photos over to the publishing house. They, in turn, selected those they wanted and sent back those they didn't want. The rejected ones never reached the photographer. Accordingly, he brought a million dollar lawsuit against the parties for the loss of the transparencies in question. The defense said that even if the transparencies were lost, it was the publishing house that lost its own materials. After all, the publishing house had employed the photographer and therefore, the photographer had no rights. The lost transparencies were eventually found and that seemed to put an end to that.

But the photographer didn't stop there. Wait a minute, he said, you owe me for holding fees, the time you kept my transparencies out of circulation.

The defendant publishing house answered that the transparencies were theirs to begin with. The photographer countered, If they were yours, why did you attempt to return them to me?

And here we have what is known as the implied contract. If it is true that the transparencies so rejected were the property of the publishing company, why return them to the photographer?

The publishing company's conduct led to the conclusion that there was indeed an implied contract between the parties whereby the photographer would get back whatever the publisher rejected. There was no decision by the courts on this matter because it was settled before trial. The photographer was paid a handsome sum for the withholding of his transparencies. (See the case of *Photo Researchers* v. *Norman, Craig and Kummel* in Chapter 8 for a court decision on holding fees.)

Now, where does this leave us? First, as to ownership, remember those ten words "As long as there is no agreement to the contrary." What are those agreements? The harshness of the law can be obviated by following certain guidelines. These guidelines are set forth in the form of sample agreements which we have seen in use (Chapter 8). Any variations of these forms are conditioned on the locale involved and the facts of the arrangement. Their intention is always to protect the photographer.

If, of course, times or conditions prevent a signed agreement, then certainly telegrams or letters setting forth the terms can be used.

No matter what form is used, remember the key points:

1. Get an agreement in writing.
2. Get it before you do the work.

TO SUMMARIZE

Where a customer employs a photographer to make pictures, the photographer, in the absence of an agreement to the contrary, has the right to retain the negatives. He may not, however, make any use of the negatives without the permission of the customer. The customer owns everything.

This does not apply to photographs taken at the expense of the photographer and for his own benefit . . . and don't forget to watch out for the implied contract.

3

Can I Use What I Take?

The answer is yes, no and maybe.

The answer is always yes when you have a proper release.

The answer is no when there is no release and the picture is used for advertising or purposes of trade.

The answer is maybe if it does not offend community sensibilities or libel an individual.

We are now in one of the most complex and certainly one of the more fascinating areas of the law: Invasion of Privacy.

When a photographer charges out to take pictures, whether for himself or for someone else, he'd better know what use he or the other party wishes to make of those pictures. For the purposes of simplification, let's separate from invasion of privacy an area known as libel. We'll discuss libel later in this section but, just for now, let's at least define the terms.

Libel is regarded as injury to one's reputation. For example, suppose you read something which is false and which undermines your integrity. That's libel . . . the printed word. (Slander is the same as libel in that it is injury to one's reputation but it is via the spoken word . . . oral.)

Invasion of privacy is an injury to one's *right* to be left alone. The right of privacy is the right to be left alone by other people (*Katz* v. *U.S.*, 88 S. Ct. 507 [1968]). You might well note that more often than not, invasion of privacy may join hands with libel in the same action. But, let's not complicate the matter more than is absolutely necessary.

One thing we should understand at the very beginning: Too often, a book on this area will start with the word "Go" and take you through an agonizing history of the law, incorporating every case and every detail. That does make for a complete, all-encompassing work. However, you the reader are not going to have the patience (and interest, generally) to snuggle up to five hundred pages of close print in one area of the law. Nobody expects you to be an expert on invasion of privacy. Volumes and volumes are being written every year and will continue to be written. Our intention here is to give you a framework, a working knowledge of this area including the latest decisions, as of the writing of this book. We are going to give you the guidelines, so that you will know where the red warning flags are.

As of now, only six states have a right of privacy statute. The other states have what is known as court-enforced regulations: otherwise known as Rule of the Court. In New York, the law rests on a statute. Why are we interested in New York law, especially since a large number of states now recognize a common-law right of privacy which is broader in scope than the statutory right in New York? Because the bulk of the law in this field is from New York. In fact, other jurisdictions will look to New York. For example, if there is a case in another jurisdiction which does not have applicable law, that jurisdiction will many times apply what has been decided here.

How did this law come about? What is it exactly? The right of privacy was never part of a common law in New York. In fact, it was not until the publication in 1890 of a law review article that privacy was even introduced and defined as an independent right and that the distinctive principles upon which it is based were formulated.

After an early case had held that there was no right of privacy enforceable at law or in equity in New York, the legislature enacted a statute giving a right of action to one whose name or picture or portrait was used without his written consent for the purposes of advertising or trade.

This is the New York Civil Rights Law which simply says that a written consent to the use of a person's name or photograph is required if either is used for advertising or trade purposes.

For those of you who like definitions spelled out, the actual statute is Section 50 of the Civil Rights Law, and it states:

A person, firm or corporation that uses for advertising purposes, or for the purposes of trade, the name, portrait or picture of any living person without having first obtained the written consent of such person, or if a minor of his or her parent or guardian, is guilty of a misdemeanor.

Violation of this section, therefore, is considered a crime.

Section 51 sets forth the civil consequences for such a violation. They include money damages and injunctive relief.

As we said before, in most jurisdictions the right of privacy exists regardless of whether the defendant uses the plaintiff's name for advertising purposes or for some other purpose. The rule in those instances is whether the use shocks one's sensibilities. This would also include advertising use.

In New York, the right rests solely on the statute; accordingly, each case alleging an invasion of privacy must turn on the question whether the use of the plaintiff's name or likeness was for purposes of trade or advertising.

Although there is no easy way to determine if an individual's privacy has been intruded upon, there are four basic rules which the courts have repeatedly stressed. Those rules, as they apply to photography, and which are followed today, are:

1. Recovery under the statute may be had if the photograph is published in or as part of an *advertisement*, or for advertising purposes; or
2. If used in connection with a work of *fiction*.
3. No recovery may be had if the photograph is published in connection with an article of current news of *immediate public interest*.
4. No recovery may be had if the article is *educational* or *informative* in character.

The case in point was *Lahiri* v. *Daily Mirror*, 162 Misc., N.Y. 776 (1937). Justice Shientag went further in setting forth what was informative or educational. He stated, "Such article includes, among others, travel stories, stories of distant places, tales of historic personages and events, the reproduction of items of past news and surveys of social conditions. These are articles educational and informative in character. As a general rule such cases are not within the purview of the statute." Now, let's break this decision down into its component parts and see how it applies.

ADVERTISING

An advertisement is the endorsement, directly or indirectly, of a product or service. If a photograph of a living individual appears in an advertisement in print, on television, or in any other visual medium without his prior written consent, the party may sue not only for damages but also for injunctive relief.

At the outset, the rule appears to be simple and clear; it's the interpretation that is sometimes confusing. To put this in perspective, let's take a look at a recent case, one which covers most of the territory settled by the law in this area.

On January 14, 1975, a decision was handed down in the Supreme Court of the State of New York in the matter of *Joe Namath* v. *Sports Illustrated* (reported in the *New York Law Journal* of January 14, 1975). The facts are as follows:

Back in 1969, *Sports Illustrated* published photographs of Namath. There was no question that the photographs were newsworthy—they were of Namath when he and his team, the Jets, defeated the Colts in the Super Bowl that year. Some three years later, *Sports Illustrated* used those same photographs in ten advertisements to promote subscriptions.

Namath sued for violation of his right of privacy and the wrongful use of his photographs without his written consent under the Civil Rights Law, Sections 50 and 51. Namath contended that in 1972, his commercial endorsements earned him in excess of several hundred thousand dollars. Therefore, *Sports Illustrated* should not be permitted to use his photographs without his written consent and certainly not without remuneration.

Sports Illustrated's defense relied primarily on a rather famous case involving the actress Shirley Booth and *Holiday* magazine, wherein *Holiday* had published a news article about a resort in the West Indies, accompanied by photographs of prominent guests (*Booth* v. *Curtis Publishing Co.*, 15 Ad 2d, 343). Miss Booth was photographed, without objection, and her picture appeared in the magazine. Six months later, it was republished as part of an advertisement for *Holiday*. The court held that there was no violation of the statute as the photograph was limited to establishing the news content and quality of the media. What this meant was that the statute could not be violated by a true and fair presentation in the news or from incidental advertising of the news medium in which the actress was properly and fairly presented.

It should be noted that there was a strong dissent by one of the justices on the basis of another case. However, that case involved a safe manufacturer and the sale of its products was for trade purposes, a classic example of what is known as collateral use. The line is thinly drawn in that it was not considered a use incidental to the dissemination of news as with the Booth matter.

This is exactly what Namath went after. He pointed out that the *Sports Illustrated* advertisement was not an incidental use but was really a collateral use: first, with the passing of time; second, the makeup of the advertisements; third, the prominent use of his name; fourth, the superimposed wording; and finally, the copy.

All well and good, but what were the real facts on this new use? Namath's photograph was printed alongside a subscription application. Promotional material appeared to one side and below the picture. The court held that it was well settled in connection with advertising that incidental use was *not* in contravention of the statute.

What this boils down to is that the court found similarities between the present case and the one between Shirley Booth and *Holiday*.

The closing remarks of the court are especially interesting:

> It is understandable that plaintiff desires payment for the use of his name and likeness in advertisements for the sale of publications in which he has appeared as newsworthy, just as he is paid for collateral endorsements of commercial products. This he cannot accomplish under the existing law of our state and nation. Athletic prowess is much admired and well paid in this country. It is commendable that freedom of speech and the press under the First Amendment transcends the right to privacy. This is so particularly when a petitioner seeks remuneration for what is basically a property right, not a right to privacy.

For those of you casting a querying look at this decision, two points should be made: (1) A photograph generally transcends state lines, and (2) The courts have shown a proclivity for bending over backwards with respect to newspapers and magazines because of the First Amendment.

As of this writing, there has not been any reversal, so that this decision still stands on the books today.

Still, the question of whether we are truly dealing with an incidental or collateral use is most interesting. The hairs are split ever so in this regard. One case in which they were split too much, at least for our blood, involved the matter of Pat Paulsen, the comedian.

In 1969, Paulsen brought an action against a firm known as Personality Posters for breach of his privacy (*Paulsen* v. *Personality Posters*, 299 NYS 2d, 501). The decision which came down said simply that a professional comedian who wages a comic campaign for the presidency of the United States, has no claim for breach of privacy against an entity that publishes and sells posters containing an enlarged comic photograph of him. You can easily fill in the facts. As far as we are concerned, we do not in any way agree with the law in this respect. It is quite obvious that Paulsen's photograph was used for trade advertising and Paulsen should have been paid for such use.

To put a cap on this area of advertising and invasion of privacy, let's take a look at two of the most recent and possibly, to date, the most famous cases involving this particular area.

One concerns the matter of *Pola Negri* v. *Schering Corporation* (333 F. Supp. 101 [1971]) and involved the clashing of two major law firms here in the District Court for the Southern District of New York.

Pola Negri, the motion picture actress, brought an action against the Schering Corporation for using a photograph of her without her consent in an advertisement for one of their pharmaceutical products.

What was the advertisement? It was a double-page, black-and-white spread which appeared in the May, 1969, issue of "MD" magazine and six other similar magazines. Two-thirds of the two-page spread was taken up with a large, full-length picture of Miss Negri as she appeared in the silent film *Bella Donna*. Miss Negri was standing, looking down at her seated, leading man. Across his lap was sprawled some other woman. Printed in large letters from the leading man's mouth were the words, "She has what they call antihistamine daze, dear." In response, from Miss Negri's mouth ballooned the words, "Has she tried POLARAMINE dexchloreniramine maleate?" ("Polaramine" is the name of the particular pharmaceutical product.)

In the right third of the two-page spread is a promotional section of several photos extolling the alleged superior virtues of the Schering product.

Schering admits it caused the advertisement to be published in the magazines and that it was done without Miss Negri's consent or authorization but, says Schering, it has no liability under the New York Civil Rights Law because (1) the photograph as it appeared in the advertisement was not a recognizable likeness of Miss Negri, and (2) the photograph of Miss Negri was not used for advertising purposes. The court first said it is true that a picture used for advertising purposes is not actionable under the statute unless it is a recognizable likeness of the plaintiff. In other words, the picture must be a clear representation of the plaintiff recognizable from the advertisement itself.

Schering tried to establish that the magazine had a limited circulation made up of medical personnel, but the court ruled that the question is whether the figure is recognizable, not the number of people who recognized it.

Look, says Schering, that photograph is not recognizable as Miss Negri today. She no longer looks as she did forty years ago when the picture was taken.

Again, said the court, no doubt Miss Negri's appearance at this writing differs substantially from what she looked like in 1922 when the picture was taken, but this is also beside the point. It doesn't matter whether or not the appearance has altered through the passage of time. She was easily recognizable as Pola Negri.

Schering said that even if the photograph were clearly recognizable, the use of it in this kind of advertisement was not really for advertising purposes. The court didn't accept this argument either, saying:

It is plain as a pikestaff that the picture is not only used to catch the eye and focus it on the advertisement, but that Miss Negri is depicted as actually recommending the Schering product. This is a blatant use of a picture purely for advertising purposes.

Now, what about a photographer who, without consent, puts a photograph of a president's widow on Christmas cards and then sends these cards to editors of various publications?

The case is *Ronald E. Galella* v. *Jacqueline Onassis* (353 F. Supp. 196 [1972]). This matter involved a number of issues wherein on one hand Galella sued Mrs. Onassis for damages for alleged false arrest, malicious prosecution and interfering with his business.

Mrs. Onassis counterclaimed charging harassment, violation of her right of privacy and so on. The trial court's decision runs from page 196 of 353 Federal Supplement to page 241. Basically, the court upheld Mrs. Onassis's position and clamped many restrictions on Galella. Some of these, it should be noted, were modified on appeal.

Insofar as invasion of privacy was concerned, the court had the problem of balancing the right of privacy against the infringement of speech; in other words, a balancing test that was responsive both to the protection of the individual's right of privacy and to the purposes of the First Amendment. Seizing on all of the matters previously discussed in this chapter and the First Amendment of the Constitution, the court tried to arrange such a balance.

The final decision, after the appeal, came down to this:

1. Galella's sending of Christmas cards to editors, which cards contained his picture on one side and Mrs. Onassis's on the other, amounted to advertising for Galella and afforded Mrs. Onassis grounds for a private right of action under Sections 50 and 51 of the New York Civil Rights Law, but

2. Galella could not properly be enjoined from taking and selling pictures of Mrs. Onassis for news coverage. Note the distinction here between advertising and news. We will be talking about news a little later on.

Now, let's turn to trade uses.

TRADE

Purposes of trade is a difficult area to define. It is not an advertisement (endorsement of a product or service). It is not news, which is immune from the privacy laws. Actually, it falls somewhere in between. It is the commercial use of a person's name or picture. How does it relate specifically to photographs? The major bulk of cases in the photographic area as they relate to purposes of trade really comes down to one issue: Is a fictionalized, nonadvertising, commercial use of a photograph made?

Try it this way. It is a photograph used in a strictly commercial sense.

The courts have held that the privacy statute in New York was not passed for the purpose of interfering with the publication of books (*Damron* v. *Doubleday*, 133 Misc. 302 [1928]).

Therefore, any reasonable use of a person's picture (such as an incidental use in a *non*fiction work relating to a subject of current interest with which he has been connected) does not constitute violation of the statutory provisions. Of course, use of a person's picture for the purposes of promoting the sale of a book has been held to constitute such a violation.

The phrase "for the purposes of trade," as used in the statute, does not include the publication of a newspaper, magazine or book which imparts truthful news or other factual information to the public (*Garner* v. *Triangle Pub.*, 97 F. Supp. 546 [1951]). Although it is admitted that a publisher sells a commodity and expects to profit from the sale of his product, he is immune from the interdict of the statute so long as he confines himself to the unembroidered dissemination of facts. It is not to be supposed, however, that the courts intended to hold truth to be a defense under the statute. If the purpose of the publication was to promote or stimulate trade in some other article or scene and it used the picture of some person without his consent, it *might*, in some instances, be actionable under the statute although it was entirely true and disclosed nothing but the facts.

The landmark case of *Dallesandro* v. *Henry Holt & Co.* (4 AD 2d, 470 [1957]) was an action by a dock worker whose photograph appeared on the cover of a book entitled *Waterfront Priest*. The dock worker was not identified by name. The court held:

> The book here involved purports to be the true story of a priest's "one-man crusade against gangsterism and terror on the New York Waterfront," and the book jacket showing the priest in earnest conversation with a longshoreman is an attempted pictorialization of the theme. It is immaterial that its manner of use and placement was designed to sell the article so that it might be paid for and read. . . .
>
> The offending book jacket is annexed to the complaint, and since it appears therefrom that the use of the picture is not actionable under the civil rights law, the complaint was properly dismissed without leave to amend.

If the book had been a total work of fiction, the result would have been different, namely a clear invasion of privacy.

CURRENT NEWS OR IMMEDIATE PUBLIC INTEREST

We must keep in mind that Americans are particularly jealous of their freedoms when it comes to press coverage. This is evident from the fact that the very first amendment to the Constitution guarantees free speech and press. The privacy statute, unknown to common law, would appear at first blush to be at variance with this concept of free speech and press. To set the record straight and to guarantee our constitutional freedoms, the courts have time and again immunized the press from the applicability of this statute. Accordingly, you should understand that no release will be necessary to protect against an invasion of privacy suit when your picture is part of a current newsworthy story or article or with respect to an educational or informative piece.

Let us give an example.

There is a chap named Murray. He sold newspapers in Queens, a borough of New York. Each year, Murray attended the St. Patrick's Day Parade. Murray was not Irish. Fair enough. A lot of non-Irish people go to the parade. Murray, however, dressed up in a green hat, green bow tie and green buttons on his green jacket and waving a green flag. Now, watching the parade, he was photographed. He didn't give his consent. He didn't even know he was being photographed. That photograph appeared on the front cover of a popular magazine. Directly above it was the title of the feature article: THE LAST OF THE IRISH IMMIGRANTS.

Naturally, it was in bold green type.

Murray was neither named in the article nor on the cover.

He sued for breach of his right of privacy under the Civil Rights Law. The matter went as high as the Court of Appeals which held that the magazine was not liable. (*Murray* v. *New York Magazine*, 27 NY 2d 406 [1971]) Why not? The court pointed out four things:

1. The article concerned itself with an event of public interest.

2. The photograph was used to spotlight the event.

3. Murray was photographed only because his presence constituted a visual participation in an event (a public one at that) which was of special note.

4. His photograph was related to the subject of the article.

But what about other magazines besides news-related publications? Especially in New York.

Even though in that state, there is some support for the view that items stressing sex or indecency give rise to a cause of action for invasion of privacy, the New York courts have on several occasions denied recovery on the ground that such articles, even if lurid, did not fall within the *statutory provision* limiting recovery to publications for the purpose of trade or advertising, or on the ground that the objectionable reference was so incidental as not to be in violation of the statute.

Know the statutory provisions of your state particularly in those states which have them. For instance, take note of the following case, again in New York.

The unauthorized use of a party's picture showing her listening to a college lecture was not actionable, under the statute, when used to illustrate a magazine article entitled "Can Marriage Be Taught?" even though questions such as "How far dare an engaged girl go?" were lettered across the picture. The court's decision here was based on the fact that there was no violation of the New York statute in using the picture "for purposes of trade or advertising" (*Vogel* v. *Hearst Corp.*, 116 NYS 2d, 905 [1952]).

Another. A magazine devoted to sensationalizing sexual abnormalities showed a picture in which an eighteen-year-old girl was sitting in a nightclub with a man, smoking and drinking, and in the background of the picture was a female impersonator. The court held no invasion of privacy under the New York statute on the ground that such magazine was not for advertising purposes or for purposes of trade (*Callas* v. *Whisper, Inc.*, 198 Misc. 829 [1950]).

Additionally, in New York, the courts held that a picture in the feature section of a newspaper showing some boys playing on a beach in the vicinity of a model wearing a swimsuit would not be held as being under the scope of advertising, pursuant to the statute.

Of course, the press privilege can work both ways. A case in Alabama not too long ago involving a newspaper which had shown a picture of a lady with her dress blown up by air jets in a fun house at a county fair was decided against the publisher on this issue. The court held that the picture was *not* to have legitimate news value since there was nothing in it to which the public was entitled to be informed (*Graham* v. *Daily Times*, 276 Ala 380 [1964]).

EDUCATIONAL AND INFORMATIVE

What about educational materials? The distinction between advertising promotional materials and genuine educational materials can indeed be tricky.

In one case, a manufacturer's instructional manual was held to be a promotional publication (even though it was certainly educational in part), because it extolled the virtues of that manufacturer's brand rather than just the class of products generally.

Corporate annual reports create a similar problem. Follow this guideline: If the picture of an employee is used in his natural working circumstances, no release is needed. If, on the other hand, the picture is used to show him pushing a product (even that of his *own* company), there is a distinct possibility of an invasion-of-privacy claim and you had better have a release. To put it another way, a release should be obtained when the principal purpose of the photograph is to show the employees themselves, while a release may not be necessary when the employee's presence is clearly incidental to the photograph involved, such as a company installation, etc. Informative articles are those of immediate public interest; i.e., politics, sports, etc. Any use of photographs in such articles is immune from the invasion of privacy statute. Articles on travel, history, social events, etc., are likewise cloaked with the veil of protection.

What then are educational or informative matters? A simple definition may be a use which is nonadvertising and nonfiction.

RULE OF COURT APPLICATIONS

As we have noted, privacy actions in nonstatute states are guided by the rules of good taste. This is not to say that satire or fair use is not permitted. In those states where there is no statute, the use of the photograph may not shock one's sensibilities. The guidelines are similar to New York's interpretation as to news, advertisements, etc.

Some examples: a city police officer in Washington, D.C., acting under the color of the law, insisted that a specific female, who had come to the police station to complain of an assault, had to be photographed in various nude and indecent positions even though she objected to undressing and maintained that her bruises would not show on any photograph. The officer proceeded to take such photographs without even calling a police-woman to be present. Thereafter, he had the photos printed and circulated among the police personnel.

The court held that the police officer's actions constituted an arbitrary intrusion upon the girl's privacy as guaranteed by the due process of the Fourteenth Amendment so as to make the officer liable in an action under the Federal Civil Rights Act (*York* v. *Story*, 324 F 2d 450 [1963]).

In another area, what happens if we decide to photograph a tourist at a Las Vegas gambling casino and we then sell the picture to a magazine which uses it in an article on gambling? Suppose we even put a caption over the picture referring to the losses of many "high rollers"? Suppose we even make reference to mob involvement in gambling operations?

Again, are we shocking the sensibilities of the public? Are we intruding upon the tourist's privacy as guaranteed under the Constitution? The answers are not that clear-cut. Generally, watch the words "The use of the photograph may not shock one's sensibilities."

PUBLIC PERSONS

The law in invasion of privacy is being interpreted similarly to the laws of libel when it comes to public persons. There is a greater latitude in the use of a picture of a public person than that of a private person. This does not mean that you can use those pictures on ads without requisite permission. The latitude is expressed in trade (fiction) areas and in those states without a statute. Let's take three major cases to demonstrate what we mean. The year was 1952. The place was Whitemarsh, Pennsylvania, the home of James Hill.

Three escaped convicts held James Hill, his wife and three children captive for nineteen hours. After their release, Mr. Hill was bombarded with offers from television companies and magazine publishers to talk about what had happened. Mr. Hill said no. In fact, to escape the constant barrage of publicity hounds, Mr. Hill and his family moved to Connecticut.

A few years later, Joseph Hayes wrote a novel called *The Desperate Hours*. It was based on the Hill incident although Hayes incorporated more violence in his story. The novel subsequently became a play, and then a film. When the play was in the try-out stages, *Life* magazine decided to do an article. It arranged to have made available the Pennsylvania home where the real incident occurred. In fact, it even transported cast members of the play to the house for photo coverage.

These scenes as photographed appeared with an article entitled "True Crime Inspires Tense Play." *Life* identified the Hill family even though Hill never agreed to the article.

Hill sued for breach of his right of privacy under the New York statute. Hill claimed that *Life* had purposely fictionalized the original incident and that neither the play nor the article was an accurate account of what really happened.

On the other side of the coin, *Life* argued that their article was news coverage.

What evolved out of this was considerable in the way of law. Hill won a decision for $175,000. This was later reduced to $30,000. Ultimately *Life* went to the United States Supreme Court. It argued that the New York right of privacy statute was unconstitutional. The court, in a 5-4 decision (*Time Inc.* v. *Hill*, 87 S. Ct. 534 [1967]), held that the statute was indeed constitutional but that a new trial must be held on the ground that liability could only be based on a finding of falsity, reckless falsity whether knowing or not.

The court considered invasion of privacy actions involving the press and "public" persons. In other words, where a private person becomes a newsworthy item by events (even those over which he has no control), he is then considered to be in the public domain.

So, what it comes down to is this: Such privacy as a person normally has, ceases when his life has ceased to be private.

The second: Warren Spahn, the great baseball pitcher, sued to prevent an unauthorized biography of himself. He claimed that the book was not a true account of his career and, therefore, a violation of his right of privacy. The publisher defended on the ground of press privilege. It argued that the suppression of such a book would be a deprivation of free speech.

The trial court awarded Spahn $10,000 on the basis that there were distortions, inaccuracies, invented dialogue and happenings out of context. The Appellate Division and the Court of Appeals affirmed the lower court's judgment. The publisher then took the matter to the U.S. Supreme Court. That court turned the decision around and sent it back to the Court of Appeals. The Supreme Court reiterated its holding in the Hill case; to wit, the New York right of privacy statute could not be used to give remedy for false reports on matters of public interest unless the reports were published with actual malice; that means, knowledge of their falsity or with reckless disregard of the truth. The case was eventually reargued. After reargument, the original judgment was reinstated. (*Spahn* v. *Messner, Inc.*, 18 L. Ed. 2d, 744 [1967]).

So, after all this hassle, what was the end result? The final decision was as follows: A public figure may have recovery for unauthorized presentation of his life, but it must be shown that the presentation is infected with material and substantial falsification and that the work was published with knowledge of such falsification or with a reckless disregard for the truth.

But, let's not stop here. Let's nail it home once and for all so that we all know where we are.

In a recent case, it was decided on a motion in the Supreme Court of the State of New York that a party must establish malice in order to prove invasion of privacy. It is the matter of *James Cagney* v. *Stein & Day* (reported in the *New York Law Journal* of January 23, 1975). It is always possible that this decision might be appealed but for the sake of analysis, let's look at how the court ruled.

Cagney we all know. Stein & Day is a major book publisher. Now, Cagney brought an action against Stein & Day for, among other things, invasion of privacy. Apparently, a particular author obtained an interview with Cagney which, according to the author, was to be used for a radio program. The author, however, then went ahead and wrote a book about Cagney. The actor claimed he would never have permitted the interview if he had known it was for a book as he was in the process of writing his own autobiography.

The part of the lawsuit in which we are interested, for the purposes of this discussion, involves invasion of privacy. The court took a long and hard look at the facts and the law which applied and came to this decision:

It is agreed that James Cagney is a public figure, and as such cannot prevent another from writing a factual and truthful account of his life, even without his consent or cooperation. The discrepancies listed by Cagney are not felt to be of such magnitude as to warrant the granting of a temporary injunction. The claim of invasion of privacy is likewise unsupported at this time as plaintiff failed to establish that the material was published with malice, that is to say that it was published with knowledge of its falsity or reckless disregard for the truth. The fact that the book may contain alleged inaccuracies does not show or prove malice.

Note specifically that last sentence. "The fact that the book may contain alleged inaccuracies does not show or prove malice."

The key here is malice. It must be shown. Otherwise what must be shown is a reckless disregard for the truth.

This should relieve the burden of the release for many people, but the question of whether to obtain a release or not is still, for most photographers, left unanswered. Many a photographer sees the signing of a release before he sees the picture he wishes to take. Sometimes, a sensational picture is lost because the photographer has been hung up over an unnecessary release; naturally, the converse is true.

Accordingly, connecting invasion of privacy with the use of a release is a problem. We come up with a number of questions. However, some decisions are easier to make than others. For example, when you are dealing with a photograph which is not to be used for advertising or promotional purposes and falls into the area of press privilege, then the decision about a release is simplified. By the same token, always consider the other side of the coin. Remember, the relation to the subject matter is important in determining the use of a release.

LIBEL

With invasion of privacy now somewhat clearer, we will consider the second section of this area known as libel.

Libel originally was considered a crime in England. It was distinguished from spoken defamation—slander—on the basis that the printed word was potentially more damaging. You see print could go much further than speech, quicker, too. Also, print was considered permanent while speech was considered "fleeting."

The American Law Institute defines libel as publication of defamatory matter "by written or printed words, by its embodiment in physical form, or by any other form of communication which has the potentially harmful qualities characteristic of written or printed words."

Libel may be an offense against a person, a corporation, a partnership, or other entities.

The landmark libel case is *The New York Times* v. *Sullivan* (84 S. Ct. 710), decided in 1964. From this case, everything falls into line—or out of line—depending upon your legal persuasion.

Libel law, it should be noted, does not require that identification be by name. It can be by inference where the name can be assumed.

It stemmed from an "editorial advertisement" entitled "Heed Their Rising Voices" in the *Times*. It was written and paid for by a group involved in obtaining equality for the American Negro. Suit was brought by L. B. Sullivan, Commissioner of Public Affairs for the City of Montgomery, Alabama, against the *Times* and four Negro clergymen who were listed among 64 persons in the advertisement. That particular ad set forth the efforts of southern Negro students to affirm their rights at the Alabama State College and it told of a "wave of terror" that greeted them. It also spoke of violence against the Rev. Martin Luther King, Jr., leader of the civil rights movement.

Commissioner Sullivan was not specifically named in the advertisement, but he claimed that because he was the Commissioner who had supervision of the Montgomery police department, anybody would quickly identify him as the person responsible for police action at the State College campus. He said too that actions against Dr. King would be immediately attributed to him by inference.

It was asserted by Sullivan, and left undisputed, that there were errors in the advertisement. In fact, the manager of the *Times* Advertising Acceptability Department said that he had not even reviewed the copy for accuracy because he had no reason to believe it false; some of the parties listed in the ad were well-known persons whose reputations he had no reason to question.

The trial jury ruled that Sullivan had indeed been libeled and awarded him $50,000. The Supreme Court of Alabama upheld the finding and judgment. But the Supreme Court of the United States reversed the decision, holding that the Alabama law was "constitutionally deficient for failure to provide the safeguards for freedom of speech and of the press that are required by the First and Fourteenth Amendments. . . ." The court said that Sullivan's claim that a paid, commercial advertisement does not deserve constitutional protection had no merit. The court further said that the question about the advertisement was whether it forfeited constitutional protection by "the falsity of some of its factual statements and by its alleged defamation of respondent."

The Constitution's guarantee of freedom of speech and press, then, protects all that is said about a public official in his public conduct except the malicious. Justice Brennan, who wrote the majority decision, stated the circumstances under which a public official could recover damages for false defamation.

> The constitutional guarantee requires, we think, a federal rule that prohibits a public official from recovering damages for a defamatory falsehood relating to his official conduct unless he proves that the statement was made with "actual malice"—that is, with knowledge that it was false or with reckless disregard of whether it was false or not.

This means only if malice were present in the publication.

But, one question arose. Did "public official" mean every person who is employed at any level?

Justice Brennan foresaw that this question would arise, and said in a footnote in the *Times* case:

> We have no occasion here to determine how far down into the ranks of government employees the "public official" designation would extend for purposes of this rule, or otherwise to specify categories of persons who would or would not be included. . . . It is enough for the present case that respondent's position as an elected city commissioner clearly made him a public official. . . .

Subsequent cases followed the *Times* doctrine in defining a public official. In one instance, the court said that the *Times* case was applicable to a person who has left public office, where public interest in the matter at issue was still substantial. In another, the court ruled that if any private citizen has, through his conduct, propelled himself into a public figure, that the *Times* rule would govern.

All well and good, and the textbooks on libel are well versed and well grounded in the famous *Times* decision. But, as you might expect, everything crumbled (or has begun to crumble) when on June 25, 1974, the Supreme Court made a decision in a libel action by a person who was *not* a public official or figure. The court held that the First Amendment does not require, as it does in cases involving public officials and figures, that the publisher of false information act with "actual malice"— knowledge that the published information was false, or with reckless disregard that it may have been. The Supreme Court took another step. It ruled that as long as the states do not impose liability without fault, they may define for themselves the appropriate standard of liability for a publisher or broadcaster of a defamatory falsehood that is injurious to a private individual. Thus, this particular case was the first one to reverse the Supreme Court's trend of providing nearly absolute First Amendment protection for the news media when sued in libel or privacy cases.

The matter is *Elmer Gertz* v. *Robert Welch, Inc.* (94 S. Ct. 2997) and by a 5-4 decision, the court overruled a long line of cases which had followed the Times/Sullivan law.

The case itself involved a libel action brought by a lawyer against a publisher of a magazine article describing the lawyer as a "Communist-fronter," "Leninist" and participant in various "Marxist" and "Red" activities.

In determining whether a plaintiff in a libel action is a "public figure" required to show "actual malice" of a publisher or broadcaster, it is preferable, said the court, to look to the nature and extent of his participation in the particular controversy giving rise to the defamation, and he should not be deemed a public personality for all aspects of his life in absence of clear evidence of general fame or notoriety in the community and the involvement in affairs of society.

Justice Powell, delivering the opinion of the court, had this to say:

> Private individuals are not only more vulnerable to injury than public officials and public figures, they are also more deserving of recovery. For these reasons, we conclude that the States should retain substantial latitude in their efforts to enforce a legal remedy for defamatory falsehood injurious to the reputation of a private individual. The extension of *The New York Times* test . . . would abridge this legitimate state interest to a degree that we find unacceptable. . . .

Now, let's examine the two latest decisions of the Supreme Court (as of this writing) and how they applied to these precedents. You will note immediately how quickly invasion of privacy and libel will interlock.

The first is *Cox Broadcasting Corporation* v. *Cohn* (95 S. Ct., 1029 [1975]). The father of a deceased rape victim brought an action against a broadcasting company (and certain others) to recover damages for invasion of his right of privacy. This invasion allegedly occurred when the broadcasting company identified the victim during television coverage of the trial of the alleged rapists.

The Supreme Court, Mr. Justice White writing the majority decision, held that the interest of privacy fades when the information involved appears on a public record and that where the television reporter based his report on notes taken during the court proceedings and obtained the rape victim's name from official court documents open to public inspection, the constitutional protection of freedom of the press barred a state from making his broadcast the basis of civil liability.

Mr. Justice Powell, who concurred in the decision, specifically cited the aforementioned Gertz case.

> Gertz is the most recent of a line of cases in which this Court has sought to resolve the conflict between the State's desire to protect the reputational interests of its citizens and the competing commands of the First Amendment. . . . In Gertz we held that the First Amendment prohibits the states from imposing strict liability for media publication of allegedly false statements that are claimed to defame a private individual. While providing the required "breathing space" for First Amendment freedoms, the Gertz standard affords the States substantial latitude in compensating private individuals for wrongful injury to reputation. . . .

The court also went into the matter of truth as a defense to a libel action. We will discuss that a few pages hence. In that respect, the Cox case covered that point in conjunction with prior cases, including Gertz. Justice Powell, again:

> I think that the constitutional necessity of recognizing a defense of truth is equally implicit in our statement of the permissible standard of liability for the publication or broadcast of defamatory statements whose substance makes apparent the substantial danger of injury to the reputation of a private citizen.

In the second important decision, we note *Cantrell* v. *Forest City Publishing Co.* (95 S. Ct. 465 [1974]). This case will be of particular interest to the photojournalist.

The facts are that, in December of 1967, Margaret Cantrell's husband was killed along with forty-three other people when the Silver Bridge across the Ohio River at Point Pleasant, West Virginia, collapsed. A reporter was assigned by the *Plain Dealer* newspaper to cover the story of the disaster. He wrote a news feature focusing on the funeral of the husband and the impact of his death on his family.

Five months later, the reporter and a photographer returned to the Point Pleasant area to write a follow-up story. The two men went to the Cantrell house where the photographer took some fifty pictures. Mrs. Cantrell was not at home and the two men spoke with the children instead. The follow-up story appeared stressing the family's abject poverty, and the deteriorating condition of their home was detailed in both text and photographs.

Mrs. Cantrell brought an action citing invasion of privacy and libel on the basis that the story contained a number of false statements. Mrs. Cantrell contended that the family was made the object of pity and ridicule and caused them to suffer outrage, mental distress, shame and humiliation.

The Supreme Court, Mr. Justice Stewart delivering the majority opinion, cited the *Time* v. *Hill* case as well as the *Times* v. *Sullivan* matter.

He reviewed the prior law that liability could be imposed only if false statements had been made with knowledge of their falsity or with reckless disregard of the truth. It was discovered at the trial that the reporter was indeed guilty of writing false statements. However, there was nothing to support any verdict against the photographer. The photographer testified that the photographs he took were fair and accurate depictions of the people and the scenes he found at the Cantrell house. He was not involved in the writing of the text and his testimony was not contradicted by any other evidence introduced at the trial.

It is particularly interesting to note the dissenting opinion of Mr. Justice Douglas:

An accident with a bridge catapulted the Cantrells into the public eye and their disaster became newsworthy. To make the First Amendment freedom to report the news turn on subtle differences between common-law malice and actual malice is to stand the Amendment on its head. Those who write the current news seldom have the objective dispassionate point of view—or the time—of scientific analysts. They deal in fast moving events and the need for "spot" reporting. The jury under today's formula sits as a censor with broad powers—not to impose a prior restraint but to lay heavy damages on the press. The press is "free" only if the jury is sufficiently disenchanted with the Cantrells to let the press be free of this damage claim.

The net effect of the Gertz case was that in a libel action by a private citizen who becomes prominent by a news event, the press no longer can turn to the qualified privilege it had under the *Times* rule. However, it must be noted that the Supreme Court maintained a few reservations in its ruling: (1) A private person may not recover punitive damages if he does not show actual malice or reckless disregard, and (2) he may not recover compensatory damages unless he can show actual harm to his reputation; that is, a monetary loss or humiliation. Accordingly, under the Gertz ruling, a private person who is involved in a matter of public interest is afforded greater protection against libel than he had before under the *Times* rule. He does not, therefore, have to establish actual malice or reckless disregard in order to recover. Simply said, the rule is that if it's a public person, you must show malice. If it's a private person, you need only show negligence. And don't forget to watch the effects of the Cox and Cantrell cases.

Libel causes damage in many ways. One of them is by ridicule. Take a photograph of a little girl eating her soup. The first week you photograph her, she has long, flowing blond hair. The second week, you get cute and do a little air-brushing, making her as bald as a billiard ball. Libelous? Possibly—it depends on whether you have more than just ridiculed the other party.

Watch yourself carefully in this area. Ridicule is obviously more than a simple joke at another's expense. But when the joke goes too deep or is too sharp, or when your photograph becomes derogatory, then ridicule reaching an actionable libel stage may have occurred.

Let us give you some examples:

Libel has been held when a joke is made out of the desertion of a bride on her wedding day. Libel has also been held when the poverty of a formerly wealthy woman was exploited.

But don't misunderstand. There is still plenty of room for satire, exaggeration, and even high levels of black comedy. For instance, a man whose obituary has appeared before his demise may feel slightly upset especially when he walks into his office the next morning. There has really been no libel. One court stated: "Death is looked for in the history of every man, and where there is notice of death that has not occurred, prematurity is the sole peculiarity."

Okay, back to pictures. Pictures, standing alone, without captions or stories with them, generally pose little danger of defamation. However, an illustration is usually accompanied by text and it is almost always that combination which carries the damaging impact.

For example, in an issue of *Tan*, a story entitled "Man Hungry" contained a picture of a professional model. The caption read: "She had a good man—but he wasn't enough. So she picked a bad one!" The cover of the magazine had the title "Shameless Love." The woman sued for libel and the court awarded her a claim for $3,000.

"There is no doubt in this court's mind that the publication libeled plaintiff," the judge wrote. "The inference to be drawn by the ordinary reading public of the magazine in question must be the criterion of measurement. . . ." A publication must be considered in its entirety, both the picture and the story which it illustrates (*Martin* v. *Johnson Pub.*, 157 NYS 2d, 409 [1956]).

Now let's briefly run down other instances of where libel can and cannot occur.

Consider a Washington, D.C., case where the court denied defendant's motion to dismiss an action for libel. A magazine article satirizing taxicab drivers used one particular driver's photograph.

Question: How would you determine liability?

Answer: Will the man in the street, in reading the story and seeing its illustrations, be justified in inferring that the text of the article applied to this particular taxicab driver? If so, libel will be sustained.

Facts: A named cafe, owned and operated by the party suing for libel, was identified as a gambling place in a photograph published in a newspaper in connection with an illustrated article about gambling in the city. The article said that the photograph of the cafe was that of the named gambling club (which, by the way, was the largest gambling place in the city) and which was conveniently located next door to the Salvation Army.

Question: Will the action be upheld?

Answer: Probably. Why? Because the name of the cafe was legible in the photograph itself and the court ruled that it is reasonable to conclude that the daily newspaper is read in the haste of daily living and that the reader can hardly be expected to search out and to recognize delicate shades in meanings and applications of the printed word and picture.

What if your subject consents to a photograph?

Be careful. As we will see in the next chapter, a consent for the most part does not apply to an offending photograph. In other words, the court will not fix upon a subject the responsibility for whatever the camera might turn out, as long as the subject did not see and approve the picture before publication, or possibly, give away the right to do so.

What we have here is another extension of what happens with the printed word. Applying the basic principles of libel to photography, the courts have said that a man may be held up as an object of ridicule, contempt or hatred by means of a picture, just as he can by words.

Remember too another aspect of libel. We are not limited to photographs solely coming out in publications. A photographer who places his stuff in the window of his studio or shows the photograph to people other than the subject can also be ruled libelous.

Now, we turn to captions on photographs. There is one case in particular worth noting, *Sydney* v. *MacFadden News* Pub., 242 NY 208 [1926]).

Here was a picture of a lady. Beneath it were the words: "Fatty Arbuckle's Lady Love " The plaintiff was a married woman and the combination of picture and caption held her up to ridicule.

The court, in its decision, said that the combination imputed an illicit relationship between the plaintiff and the comedian.

The same result was had where a picture of a onetime wrestling champion was captioned, "_____, Wrestler, Not Fundamentally Different From The Gorilla In Physique." It wasn't quite an illicit relationship here but the result was the same. You can imagine where the wrestler's picture was.

Here's another one. A newspaper publishes next to photographs of four boys under the headline: "Slain School Girl Vanishes With Someone In Cadillac." Below the picture are these words: "These four acquaintances of murdered _____ _____ are cooperating with police in seeking clues that may lead to the girl's slayer." Now, five lines below the pictures, is another headline: "Four Youths Held; 60 To 70 Friends Face Grilling." Libel? Well, frankly, it's a question of fact whether the photographs, captions and headings, all combined, could give the impression that the four boys are the same ones being held. This could become a jury decision.

Thus, it is highly important that caution be exercised whenever captions are placed next to photographs. A seemingly innocent caption may often be offensive. For example a photograph of two women standing close together. One of them is trying to light a cigarette. The other, a rather heavy-set woman, looks as though she is trying to offer some protection from the wind. The caption the photographer wants to use? "Windbreaker," of course. Libelous?

Most libel cases actually involve the combination of photographs with articles. For example, a newspaper publishes an article about cheating car dealers. Next to the article is a picture of a man who is not a car dealer. Obviously, a wrong inference about this man can be drawn from the use of the photograph next to such an article.

The same thing applies to photographs of places. An article in a newspaper on investigating illegal banking procedures was made more delicious by the photograph of a bank not involved in the investigation. Libelous?

Even a retouched photograph must be scrutinized. You must realize that a retouched photograph may be objectionable to the subject of it even though the original photograph was not. Case in point? Well, you'll see it in the next chapter on releases about the good-looking lady in bed reading a book. As a practical approach, always caption your photographs properly so that a "legal" shot does not become actionable as libel because of an overzealous copywriter.

Okay, then, how do you watch out for libel? Difficult, but like everything else we have discussed thus far, not impossible. Just have a good working knowledge of this whole area of invasion of privacy and libel and know where the parameters are. And above all, remember that when all is said and done, libel does have a pretty good defense . . . and that is truth. Truth is always a defense in libel.

TO SUMMARIZE

Use of photographs in the news, educational, current illustrative areas, generally does not require a release. Use of photographs in advertising and for purposes of trade does require a release. The best rule, however, is to acquire a release, if possible, under all circumstances. Why? Because you do not know what use will be made of the photograph that was taken.

As to libel, the best way to protect yourself from liability is to caption properly every photograph and print that you make. Then, the ultimate user of the photograph, if he miscaptions or if he deletes your caption and applies his own, will be solely responsible for any libel which may eventually occur.

Realize that this summary is general in nature and, in any area of confusion, check with your own attorney. This area is the one in which most photographers are sued. Be careful!

4

What Kind of Release Do I Need?

Whenever a person's name, portrait, or photograph is used without written consent, the question of the possibility of an invasion-of-privacy action arises. This is where the release comes into play.

First, what is a release?

It is a piece of paper signed by the party to be photographed to the effect that said party has given his or her consent to such photograph being taken and also for its use. The function of a release then is to provide that necessary written consent.

In New York, for example, there is a Civil Rights Law (as we have defined in the preceding chapter) which requires a written consent for the use of a person's name or photograph in advertising or promotion. In other words, the name, portrait or picture of any living person may not be used for advertising purposes or for purposes of trade without prior written consent.

Let's clear up one common misconception. Is compensation necessary for a release to be effective? Do you have to pay the other party or does the other party have to pay you? The answer is a big, fat NO. Only consent is required. Must it always be in writing? No, again. Some states only require oral consent. But try to prove it! The suggestion is to *get it in writing*.

Most of the professional photographers whose photographs are to be used in a commercial venture (i.e., for advertising and promotional uses) generally obtain releases as a matter of good business practice. But sometimes photographers do things back-wards. They fail to obtain at the time the photographs are shot, then have to run around after them at a later date. Many times the release itself leaves much to be desired, as when there is no connection between the release that is signed and the specific photograph to which it is supposed to apply.

What do we mean? Well, it is obtaining a release without specifying what it is that is being released. There have been in-stances where models have challenged releases later on.

This can be avoided (a) by obtaining the release at the con-clusion of the photographic session and (b) dating both the re-lease, and the negatives.

Remember one thing: the defense of consent poses a number of difficulties anyway. To make a defense stand up, it must be pleaded and proved. Therefore, keep this rule in mind: the con-sent must be as broad as the alleged invasion.

A case in point involved a young man who had consented to have his picture taken in a doorway of a store, supposedly dis-cussing the World Series. But, the photograph was used in a detective magazine to illustrate a story on gangs. The young man could easily recover for damages on the basis that consent to one thing is not consent to another. Accordingly, when a photograph is used for a purpose not intended by the person who consented, that person may be able to collect damages for invasion of privacy, if the other elements of such a suit are present.

What kind of release then should you use? There is no stan-dard form of release for professional models. Different pho-tographers use different forms. Many of the forms we have seen in current use are less than adequate. Why? Because basically we are dealing with an important American right—the right to perpetuate ourselves in error. If a photographer is to have the right to use a photograph for any legitimate purpose whatso-ever, that should be made explicit in the release. Conversely, if the photograph is to be used only for a specific purpose, that purpose should be clearly defined.

Try this candid camera scenario:

You take a picture of an eight-year old girl sipping a bowl of soup in a restaurant.

It's for an advertising campaign. The shutter snaps. The bulb flashes. The little girl looks up. The big barrel-chested man next to her gives out with a "Hey."

What do you do?

Well, first off, you smile back and then reach for your back pocket.

In one smooth motion, you whip out a single sheet of paper. When in doubt, whip it out.

"Are you her father?" you say to the barrel-chested man.

He nods.

You shove the paper under his nose. "Here. Have her sign this."

He stares at it:

RELEASE

For valuable consideration (receipt of which is hereby acknowledged), I hereby give Peter Photographer the absolute, irrevocable right and permission, forever and throughout the world, in connection with the photographs he has taken of me, or in which I may be included with others, the following:

(a) The right to use and reuse, in any manner at all, said photographs, in whole or in part, either by themselves or in conjunction with other photographs, in any medium and for any purposes whatsoever, including, without limitation, all promotional and advertising uses, and other trade purposes, as well as using my name in connection therewith, if he so desires; and

(b) The right to copyright said photographs in his own name or in any other name that he may select.

I hereby forever release and discharge Peter Photographer from any and all claims, actions and demands arising out of or in connection with the use of said photographs, including, without limitation, any and all claims for invasion of privacy and libel.

This release shall inure to the benefit of the assigns, licensees and legal representatives of Peter Photographer, as well as the party(ies) for whom he took said photographs.

I represent that I am over the age of twenty-one years and that I have read the foregoing and fully and completely understand the contents hereof.

Date: _____(L.S.)

Witnessed by: _____

_____

(Address)

"What is it?" he asks.

"A release," you answer.

He blinks. He reaches into his pocket. Out comes an enormous, shiny, black . . . pen.

"Where does she sign?" he says.

Aha. "Right here," you point, grinning.

The pen descends, then stops in midair.

"Wait a minute," he says. "She can't sign this."

Your Leica sinks. You sit down.

"Why not?"

"'Cause my kid is under age."

What do you do now?

Simple. You just add the following to the bottom of the release and have him sign where indicated:

I represent that I am the father of Betty Beautiful, the above-named model. For value received, I hereby consent to the foregoing on her behalf.

Dated: _____(L.S.)

Witnessed by: _____

_____   (Address)

It should be pointed out that most model releases run to the photographer. However, if the model is engaged by an advertising agency, the release should also run to the agency. Full protection all the way around is essential. Will a release help you if a picture is distorted? What do we mean? Well, suppose you later take that picture of the little girl and airbrush all her hair out. Will the release her father signed protect you?

There has been much in the way of cases involving the use of photographs in other ways by retouching and distorting the image. Most of these cases fall into the area known as libel, which we previously discussed, but insofar as releases are concerned, consider the following case. This is one of the more famous cases in this area and which everyone researching the photographic field points to, *Russel* v. *Marboro Books*, 183 NYS 2d, 8 (1959).

Here are the facts. A New York fashion model posed for an advertisement to promote a book club. The photograph showed her in bed reading a book. There is no nudity involved. She had signed this release:

The undersigned hereby irrevocably consents to the unrestricted use by (the name of the photographer) . . . advertisers, customers, successors and assigns, of my name, portrait or picture, for advertising purposes or purposes of trade, and I wave the right to inspect or approve such completed portraits, pictures, or advertising matter used in connection therewith. . . .

The model claimed that her job in the world of fashion modeling involved her portraying an "intelligent, refined, well-bred, pulchritudinous, ideal young wife and mother in artistic settings and socially approved situations." Her understanding of the arrangement was that the picture was to depict a wife in bed with her "husband" (a model) beside her, reading. The book company did use the pictures in an advertisement, with the caption "For People Who Take Their Reading Seriously."

Thus far, any problem that you can see?

No? You're right. No problem.

The book company, however, sold the photograph to a manufacturer of bed sheets. This manufacturer enjoyed a reputation for publishing sexy ads. The photo was retouched so that the title of the book which our fashion model was reading, became "Clothes Make the Man," a book which had been banned as pornographic.

Underneath the photograph was an invitation to the readers to supply a caption in order to advertise bed sheets.

The bed sheet company explained that they attempted to write a caption but all they could come up with were captions like "Lost Weekend," "Knight Errant," "Lost Between the Covers" and "You Can't Go Wrong with a Springmaid Sheet."

The fashion model did not lie still for this one. She sued for $50,000, charging she had not consented to the subsequent use of the photograph and that she had been damaged professionally (not to mention her social standing) by an advertisement which invited readers to play around with her moral character. Springmaid counterpunched. They felt the release she signed was sufficiently broad to permit them to use the photograph as they saw fit.

So, what do you think now?

The court held in this case that the fashion model had an action for invasion of privacy and libel despite the unlimited release she had signed. Such a release, the court reasoned, would not stand up "if the picture were altered sufficiently in situation, emphasis, background, or context . . . liability would accrue where the content of the picture has been so changed that it is substantially unlike the original. In this aspect of the case, I speak of content of the picture as used, not the purpose or extent of its use."

In other words, said the court, although the model consented in writing to the use of her portrait for advertising purposes by others and agreed that she would forego inspection and approval of the completed material when ready for publication, it did not follow that the consent signed would go beyond its wording so as to exculpate, as a matter of law, the dissemination of all types of altered pictures or of libelous material.

Accordingly, it is quite important to include in your release all those uses which might be contemplated or agreed to.

How do we do this? Try this form of release:

RELEASE

In consideration of my engagement as a model, upon the terms hereinafter stated, I hereby grant to you forever, your assigns, licensees and legal representatives, and their assigns and licensees, including, without limitation, those for whom you are acting, and those acting with your authority and permission, the absolute and irrevocable right and permission to copyright and use and reuse, all photographs of me or in which I may be included, whether in whole or in part, and whether as a composite picture or distorted in character or form, without restriction of any kind. This grant shall also include the right to change or alter, from time to time, all such photographs, whether in conjunction with my own or a fictitious name, or whether made through any media or process at my studios or elsewhere for art, advertising, trade, promotion or any other purpose whatsoever.

I also consent to and grant the right for the use of any printed matter in conjunction with the foregoing.

I hereby waive any and all rights which I may have to inspect or approve the finished product or products or the advertising copy or printed matter or any other matter that may be used in connection therewith or the use to which it may be applied. I hereby release, discharge and agree to defend and save harmless, you, your legal representatives, licensees and assigns, and all parties acting under your permission or with authority from you or those for whom you are acting, from any liability of whatsoever kind, by reason of any distortion, alteration, blurring, optical illusion, changes or use in composite or other form, whether intentional or not, which may occur or be produced in the making of said photograph or in any processing thereof, as well as any publication thereof even though it may subject me to humiliation, riducule, scandal or any other indignity of whatsoever kind.

I hereby warrant and represent that I am of full age and have every right to contract in my own name with respect to the above.

I further warrant that I have read this release and the terms hereof, prior to its execution, and that I am fully familiar with the contents hereof.

Dated: _____(L.S.)

_____

Witness

(Address)

This is what is known as a "Blockbuster" release and if you can get this one signed, you should be on fairly solid footing should anything go wrong.

The next area to consider is the property release. This means exactly what it says: A release to a photographer for photographing certain property. Although most states don't recognize invasion of privacy actions in connection with a piece of property, other areas of the law may make such a use actionable.

Here's the kind of release in use today:

PROPERTY RELEASE

For good and valuable consideration, herein acknowledged, the undersigned being the legal owner of, or having the right to permit the taking and use of photographs of certain property designated as _____, does hereby grant to Peter Photographer, his agents, assigns, licensees and legal representatives, the full right to use such photographs (and to copyright same) for all purposes, including, without limitation, for purposes of advertising, trade and promotion.

The undersigned also consents to the use of any printed matter in conjunction therewith.

The undersigned hereby waives any right that he may have to inspect or approve the finished product or products or the advertising copy or printed matter that may be used in connection therewith or the use to which it may be applied.

The undersigned hereby releases, discharges and agrees to defend and save harmless Peter Photographer, his legal representatives, licensees and assigns, and all persons acting under his or their permission or authority, or those for whom he or they are acting, from any liability by reason of any blurring, distortion, alteration, optical illusion, or use in composite form, whether intentional or otherwise, that may occur or be produced in the making of said picture or in any processing thereof, as well as any publication thereof, even though it may subject the undersigned to humiliation, ridicule, scandal or any other indignity.

The undersigned hereby warrants and represents that he has the right to contract in his own name in the above regard. The undersigned states further that he has read the above authorization, release and agreement, prior to its execution, and that he is fully familiar with the contents thereof.

Dated: _____(L.S.)

Witness:

_____   _____
                              (Address)

Let's turn to the film and television areas. You all know that documentary films often include individuals who are not professional models.

The release form used by motion picture companies reflects the wide scope necessary. In fact, this type of form is used even for special premieres where the company desires to film the "gala opening" of its latest opus and then utilize the footage later on in its advertising.

Date:_____

The undersigned hereby grants to _____, its successors, assigns and licensees, the irrevocable right, license and privilege, to use, record, dub, amplify, reproduce, perform, represent, exhibit, televise, transmit, exploit and simulate the undersigned's name, likeness, photograph, voice and musical and other performances, throughout the world, in any manner and form and by any method and process and through any media now or hereafter known or devised, in and in connection with the motion picture presently entitled ———————————, to be produced or released by ———————————, its successors, assigns or licensees, and in the advertising, publicity and exploitation thereof.

Witness:

———————————(L.S.)

———————————

(Address)

Simple. Yet, it does the trick.

The television area, though, has more nuances to it and a typical release for this area would be as follows:

To:

Gentlemen:

1. I hereby agree to your recording my appearance and participation on your television program presently entitled

———————————.

2. I acknowledge that you are or will be the sole owner of all rights in and to this television program and the recordings thereof. You shall have the right, among other things, to telecast the program or the recordings thereof one or more times, on a sustaining or commercial basis, over any station or stations that you own, as well as over any affiliated stations licensed by you.

3. I understand that I shall receive no compensation for my appearance on and participation in the program.

(Or put in compensation if applicable)

4. You shall have the right to use and license others to use my name, portrait, picture and biographical material to publicize and advertise the program, but not as an endorsement of any product or service.

5. I agree to hold you and any other parties harmless against any claim, liability, loss or damage (including attorney's fees) caused by or arising from my appearance on the program, of any utterance made by me or material furnished by me in connection with my participation therein.

Dated:

Very truly yours,

Confirmed:

———————————

———————————

(Address)

So, where does all this leave us?

TO SUMMARIZE

When it comes down to deciding whether a release is needed or not, the photographer should understand clearly that it is the manner and context of the use of a person's photograph which determine whether that person's privacy has been invaded; it is not always the nature of the photograph itself. The point is this: If you don't know what the ultimate purpose of the photograph is going to be, then get a release and make sure it's the proper form for the purpose. Better to be safe than sorry, as the old cliché goes.

Finally, when dealing with releases, keep in mind that you are getting into the area of invasion of privacy and libel.

You now should know whether or not you need a release and how you can use what you take. The next important factor to consider is what to do with what you take and that means the area known as copyright.

5

Can I Copyright
What I Take?

It may have been Mark Twain, or perhaps Will Rogers, who said that whenever the U.S. Copyright Law was to be reviewed or altered, then all the idiots assembled in Washington.

The fact is that the law of copyright is probably the most confused, maligned, complicated and generally abused of the legal areas. There are countless books written about the subject and innumerable courses taught in the universities. It is apparent that incorporating the copyright law and all of the pertinent analyses in this publication would scarcely be practical. The intention here is to offer a general guideline, upon which you can base sound decisions. We will try to show you how the law applies to photography and what you can and cannot do with it.

The present copyright law dates back to 1909. That's right. Notwithstanding certain subsequent modifications, the law is 66 years old at this writing. For no other reason than the vital changes in technology during this period, this law should be retired. In fact, new proposals are now before the Congress after more than a decade of negotiations. Hopefully, in our lifetime, we will witness the birth of a newer and saner copyright law.

The law we are referring to is the United States Copyright Act.

Basically, it grants protection against copying, without permission, the copyrighted work of another, or using that work to create a substantial duplication.

This is the guts of the copyright law.

How does one protect his work?

The U.S. Copyright Act provides for the registration of photographs. Photography, when it comes to copyright, is not chopped liver. It has already been adjudicated as being eligible for copyright protection. For example, take a photograph of a person. The photographer poses the subject, selects and arranges the costume, draperies, and other accessories, adjusts the lights and shade, and suggests and evokes the expression. "This must be deemed a work of art and its maker an author, inventor or designer of it, within the meaning and protection of the copyright statute" (*Burrow-Giles Lithographic Co.* v. *Sarony*, 4 S. Ct. 279).

But besides the registration in Washington, there is what is known as common law copyright.

In the area of photographs, suppose you have a picture of your red telephone sitting on a yellow toaster. Without doing a thing, that photograph is automatically protected under the common law for the time it remains unpublished—even to perpetuity. So long as that photograph is not published, you own the common law copyright in it and no one may use or copy it without your permission.

"So long as it remains unpublished?" you ask. What does "unpublished" mean?

To publish a work means to make it available to the public in some way, usually by the sale or public distribution of copies. In other words, "publication" in the copyright sense means dissemination of the work among the public in such a way as to justify the belief that the distribution took place with the intention of making the work available to the public at large.

Performance is not considered publication. For example, if you have an exhibition in a gallery or museum, chances are such exhibition would not be considered a publication of your work. However, if there were no restriction on taking photographs or copying your work in any other way, then there would be a publication and the common law copyright might be lost.

One little caveat. We used the word "distribution" above. A *sale* of your work does not have to take place to constitute publication. Mere distribution of copies means publication even though no sales are being made.

Another way to achieve copyright protection for unpublished photographs is through the medium known as an unpublished statutory copyright.

What this means is that you register your photograph in the Copyright Office in Washington, D.C. It is mailed to Washington along with an application and a filing fee—we'll tell you how to do that a little later in this section.

There are advantages and disadvantages for both types of copyright for unpublished photographs. The main difference is that the common law type is often difficult to prove.

How do you show that the work was first made by you to obtain common law protection? That's one of the problems but, once 'established, you receive protection in perpetuity.

The statutory copyright is good for a period of twenty-eight years (with a renewal right of twenty-eight years), but its proof is a lot easier if you have the photograph registered in the copyright office as soon as it is taken.

A renewal, incidentally, is not considered an extension; it is a whole new copyright. Watch closely for the renewal date for once a copyright expires, it is lost, never to be regained.

The third type is the published statutory copyright.

This means exactly what it says: A copyright registration of the photograph once it reaches the publication stage. The term of protection is the same as the unpublished statutory kind: twenty-eight years with a renewal right of an additional twenty eight-years. Renewals of copyrights can be obtained during the last twelve-month period of the initial term.

It should be noted that the bill presently before the Congress would change this to the life of the author or photographer plus fifty years. Most European countries already have this in effect.

Our neighbor to the north, Canada, is presently revising its copyright act too. The term of copyright in Canada is fifty years from the making of the original photograph.

We mentioned the European countries. You should understand that there are three specific international treaties relating to a copyrighted work. Signatories to the Universal Copyright Convention include the United States, Canada, England and other industrialized countries. The Berne Convention does not include the United States but includes most of the European countries and runs from Argentina and Australia to Uruguay and

Yugoslavia. The Buenos Aires Convention covers countries in South America. Some countries are members of several or all the conventions. In fact, Canada and many other countries are signatories to both Berne and UCC. One of the most important factors here is to make sure a copyright legend is included on all your work. The ideal copyright line, and the one which most photographers have made up in stamp form, is as follows:

Copyright © by Priscilla Photographer (Insert year of first
publication)
All Rights Reserved

Some have questioned the use of the words "All Rights Reserved." Interestingly enough, those words place the work within the copyright protection of the Buenos Aires Convention.

What if you don't copyright your photograph? Simply this—the failure to copyright can result in a loss of protection; in other words, your work will be thrown into the public domain and become available to anyone without your permission.

This allegedly happened recently with a monumental work of Picasso's in Chicago. Anyone and his sister-in-law is now free to make miniature reproductions of the work, place photographs of it on postcards, or dream up any other copying technique without compensation.

A work may fall into the public domain for various reasons, among which are improper notices and wrong dates. An example might be publishing the photograph in 1974 but copyrighting it in 1975. In effect, the attempted copyright to protect the work followed its publication when it was unprotected. Consequently, by law this work fell into the public domain and could never again be protected. To nail down this question of publication, you should understand that publication means the distribution of copies of the photograph, for sale or otherwise, and not necessarily the reproduction of the photograph in a book, newspaper or magazine.

Why? Because in the latter case, the photograph is generally protected by the copyright of the work in which it appears, or may be copyrighted separately, either as a "book," a "print" or a "contribution."

There has been a diversity of opinion on this last point. A number of "experts" in the copyright field question whether true protection is afforded by the book's copyright. To this argument, we can only cite the landmark decision of *Goodis* v. *United Artists et al* (425 F2d 397—2d Cir.—1970).

Photography is not specifically involved here but the concept behind this ruling is important to understand.

Question: does a magazine publisher who acquires only the right to serialize a novel before it is published in book form have such an interest in the work that notice of copyright in the publisher's name will protect the copyright of the author of the novel?

The controlling facts are that in 1945 David Goodis wrote a book entitled *Dark Passage*. It dealt with a man's escape from a penitentiary to solve a murder of which he had been convicted.

Goodis made arrangements for the book to be printed in April, 1966. Before the book was published, Goodis granted Curtis Publishing the right to serialize the novel in *The Saturday Evening Post*. The book publisher agreed to postpone publication of the book until October, 1946, and *Dark Passage* was then first published in eight installments of *The Saturday Evening Post* from July 20 to September 7, 1946. Each issue contained a single copyright notice in the magazine's name as provided by the Copyright Act. There was no notice in Goodis's own name. Remember too, that copyright in a book cannot be obtained *until* the book is published. There is no unpublished statutory copyright for books, as there is for photographs. There ensued a number of problems relating to the motion picture which was later produced and a television series based on the property. The facts relating to those projects are really not germane to what we are considering. Suffice it to say, an action for copyright infringement was instituted and the defendants defended on the grounds that the work had fallen into the public domain by the serialization by Curtis. All three judges in the United States Court of Appeals concurred that where a magazine has purchased the right of first publication under circumstances which showed that the author had no intention to donate his work to the public, copyright notice in the magazine's name was sufficient to obtain a valid copyright on behalf of the beneficial owner, the author. The Court found it difficult to believe that there was any intention by Goodis to surrender the fruits of his labor. The Court believed that the issue of protecting the author's interest was supported by the Copyright Act and by common sense.

The Court also noted that the proposed general revisions of the copyright law would also substantiate its findings. What are these proposed revisions? (1) the author of a literary work which is published for the first time in a "collective work," such as a periodical, holds a copyright distinct from that in the collective work as a whole; (2) that first publication in a collective work under a general copyright notice in the name of the periodical publisher is sufficient to secure the author's copyright in the work; and (3) that where the person named in the copyright notice applicable to a collective work is not the owner of the copyright in a separate contribution which appears in the collective work without its own notice, the case is treated simply as one with an error in the name in the notice, such error not affecting the validity or ownership of the copyright.

The Court also took into consideration modern business practices. Today, many magazines market new writings in serial form. It should be expected that serialization will often be the "first publication" of a work, since much of the value of such an arrangement to the periodical lies in reaching magazine readers before the complete book has been released.

In conclusion, Chief Judge Lumbard wrote: "That such an arrangement between Curtis and Goodis is in the nature of a 'partial assignment' is no reason to require a different result. This circuit 30 years ago understood the desirability of recognizing partial assignments. *Houghton Mifflin Co.* v. *Stackpole Sons, Inc.*, 104 F 2d, 306 (1939). Where the question is the interest needed to obtain copyright, we reiterate that the important considerations are the intention of the parties to obtain copyright and the adequacy of notice to the public; the characterization of the publisher as assignee or licensee is secondary."

How then is a photograph copyrighted? How is it registered?

On page 62 is a form of registration for a photograph. Copies may be obtained from the Copyright Office in Washington. The procedure for filing is quite simple. The form is filled in and two copies of the photograph (one copy if an unpublished registration is applicable), along with a $6 filing fee, is sent to Washington. It should be specifically noted that for registration purposes, every photograph should have a title, which must appear on the photograph. But, a warning! Remember Chapter 2? Determine who owns the photograph. The question of ownership is indeed sticky.

One way is to have the copyright in a photograph which is to be owned by you but which rests with another party assigned over to you. We went through something similar in the Goodis case. In that connection, you may find the following form of copyright assignment suitable:

ASSIGNMENT

KNOW ALL MEN BY THESE PRESENTS, that for good and valuable consideration, receipt of which is hereby acknowledged, the undersigned _____, as copyright owner in the certain photograph entitled "_____" (hereinafter referred to as "said work"), which was registered for copyright in the Copyright Office of the United States of America as an *(un) published* work by and in the name of _____ on _____, Number _____, hereby confirms all of the rights held anywhere in the world by _____ under and pursuant to the certain agreement dated_____ between_____ and _____, which said agreement being by this reference thereto hereby made a part hereof; and also hereby confirms, grants, and assigns to said _____, his successors and assigns, all rights, licenses, privileges and interests in said work during the original term of said copyright and any renewals or extensions thereof; and hereby also warrants that the undersigned has not heretofore made any grant, encumbrance or other disposition to others of any right, title or interest in said work hereby confirmed, granted and assigned.
IN WITNESS WHEREOF, the undersigned has caused these presents to be executed this_____day of _____, 19_____.

Notarization

If you are dealing with an agreement involving a more complicated arrangement, you could protect yourself by making sure that the agreement contains a grant clause which will give you the copyright in the photograph. An example of such a grant clause is as follows:

JOE JONES, as beneficial owner thereof, hereby assigns to PRISCILLA PHOTOGRAPHER, absolutely, his entire right,

Application
for Registration of a Claim to Copyright
in a photograph

FORM J

REGISTRATION NO.

DO NOT WRITE HERE
JFO   JF   JP   JU

CLASS

J

Instructions: Make sure that all applicable spaces have been completed before you submit the form. The application must be **SIGNED** at line 9. For published works the application should not be submitted until after the date of publication given in line 4 (a), and should state the facts which existed on that date. For further information, see page 4.

Pages 1 and 2 should be typewritten or printed with pen and ink. Pages 3 and 4 should contain exactly the same information as pages 1 and 2, but may be carbon copies.

Mail all pages of the application to the Register of Copyrights, Library of Congress, Washington, D.C. 20559, together with:

(a) If unpublished, one complete copy of the work and the registration fee of $6.

(b) If published, two copies of the best edition of the work and the registration fee of $6.

Make your remittance payable to the Register of Copyrights.

1. Copyright Claimant(s) and Address(es): Give the name(s) and address(es) of the copyright owner(s). For published works the name(s) should ordinarily be the same as in the notice of copyright on the copies deposited. If initials are used in the notice, the name should be the same as appears elsewhere on the copies.

Name _____

Address _____

Name _____

Address _____

2. Title of Photograph: _____
(Give the title as it appears on the copies; each copy deposited should bear an identifying title, which may be descriptive)

_____

3. Author: Citizenship and domicile information must be given. Where a work was made for hire, the employer is the author. The citizenship of organizations formed under U.S. Federal or State law should be stated as U.S.A.

If the copyright claim is based on new matter (see line 5) give information about the author of the new matter.

Name _____ Citizenship _____
(Name of country)

Domiciled in U.S.A. Yes ____ No ____ Address _____

➤➤ NOTE: | Leave all spaces of line 4 blank **unless your work has been PUBLISHED.** | ◄◄

4. (a) Date of Publication: Give the complete date when copies of this particular photograph were first placed on sale, sold, or publicly distributed. The date when the photograph was made or the date when copies were reproduced should not be confused with the date of publication. NOTE: The full date (month, day, and year) must be given.

_____
(Month)   (Day)   (Year)

(b) Place of Publication: Give the name of the country in which this particular photograph was first published.

_____

➤➤ NOTE: | Leave all spaces of line 5 blank **unless the instructions below apply to your work.** | ◄◄

5. Previous Registration or Publication: If a claim to copyright in any substantial part of this work was previously registered in the U.S. Copyright Office in unpublished form, or if a substantial part of the work was previously published anywhere, give requested information.

Was work previously registered? Yes _____ No _____ Date of registration _____ Registration number _____

Was work previously published? Yes _____ No _____ Date of publication _____ Registration number _____

Is there any substantial **NEW MATTER** in this version? Yes _____ No _____ If your answer is "Yes," give a brief general statement of the nature of the **NEW MATTER** in this version. (New matter may consist of compilation, abridgment, editorial revision, and the like, as well as additional pictorial material.)

_____

_____

EXAMINER

Complete all applicable spaces on next page

6. If registration fee is to be charged to a deposit account established in the Copyright Office, give name of account:

---

7. Name and address of person or organization to whom correspondence or refund, if any, should be sent:

Name _____ Address _____

8. Send certificate to:

(Type or print name and address)

Name _____

Address _____
(Number and street)

_____
(City)   (State)   (ZIP code)

9. Certification:

(Application not acceptable unless signed)

I CERTIFY that the statements made by me in this application are correct to the best of my knowledge.

(Signature of copyright claimant or duly authorized agent)

Application Forms

Copies of the following forms will be supplied by the Copyright Office without charge upon request:

Class A	Form A—Published book manufactured in the United States of America.
Class A or B	Form A–B Foreign—Book or periodical manufactured outside the United States of America (except works subject to the ad interim provisions of the copyright law).
	Form A–B Ad Interim—Book or periodical in the English language manufactured and first published outside the United States of America.
Class B	Form B—Periodical manufactured in the United States of America.
	Form BB—Contribution to a periodical manufactured in the United States of America.
Class C	Form C—Lecture or similar production prepared for oral delivery.
Class D	Form D—Dramatic or dramatico-musical composition.
Class E	Form E—Musical composition the author of which is a citizen or domiciliary of the United States of America or which was first published in the United States of America.
	Form E Foreign—Musical composition the author of which is not a citizen or domiciliary of the United States of America and which was not first published in the United States of America.
Class F	Form F—Map.
Class G	Form G—Work of art or a model or design for a work of art.
Class H	Form H—Reproduction of a work of art.
Class I	Form I—Drawing or plastic work of a scientific or technical character.
Class J	Form J—Photograph.
Class K	Form K—Print or pictorial illustration.
	Form KK—Print or label used for an article of merchandise.
Class L or M	Form L–M—Motion picture.
Class N	Form N—Sound recording.
•	Form R—Renewal copyright.
•	Form U—Notice of use of copyrighted music on mechanical instruments.

FOR COPYRIGHT OFFICE USE ONLY	
Application received	
One copy received	
Two copies received	
Fee received	
Renewal	

Certificate
Registration of a Claim to Copyright
in a photograph

FORM J

REGISTRATION NO.

DO NOT WRITE HERE

CLASS J

This Is To Certify that the statements set forth on this certificate have been made a part of the records of the Copyright Office. In witness whereof the seal of the Copyright Office is hereto affixed.

Register of Copyrights
United States of America

NOT VALID WITHOUT
COPYRIGHT OFFICE
IMPRESSION SEAL

1. Copyright Claimant(s) and Address(es):

Name _____

Address _____

Name _____

Address _____

2. Title of Photograph: _____
(Title of photograph as it appears on the copies)

_____

3. Author:

Name _____ _____ Citizenship _____
(Name of country)

Domiciled in U.S.A. Yes ____ No ____ Address _____ _____

4. (a) Date of Publication:

_____
(Month) (Day) (Year)

(b) Place of Publication:

_____
(Name of country)

5. Previous Registration or Publication:

Was work previously registered? Yes _____ No _____ Date of registration _____ Registration number _____

Was work previously published? Yes _____ No _____ Date of publication _____ Registration number _____

Is there any substantial **NEW MATTER** in this version? Yes _____ No _____ If your answer is "Yes," give a brief general statement of the nature of the **NEW MATTER** in this version.

_____

_____

Complete all applicable spaces on next page

EXAMINER

6. Deposit account:

---

7. Send correspondence to:

Name .... Address ....

8. Send certificate to:

(Type or
print   **Name**
name and
address)   **Address**

(Number and street)

(City)   (State)   (ZIP code)

Information concerning copyright in photographs

When to Use Form J. Form J is appropriate for unpublished and published photographs.

What Is a "Photograph"? This category (Class J) includes photographic prints and filmstrips, slide films, and individual slides.

—*Reproductions.* Reproductions of photographs prepared by photolithography and other mechanical processes are generally regarded as "prints" rather than "photographs" and, when published, should be submitted for registration on Form K.

—*Contributions to Periodicals.* When a photograph is first published with a separate copyright notice in a magazine or newspaper, it is regarded as a "contribution to a periodical," registrable on Form BB.

Duration of Copyright. Statutory copyright begins on the date the work was first published, or, if the work was registered for copyright in unpublished form, copyright begins on the date of registration. In either case, copyright lasts for 28 years, and may be renewed for a second 28-year term.

Unpublished photographs

How to Register a Claim. To obtain copyright registration, mail to the Register of Copyrights, Library of Congress, Washington, D.C. 20559, one complete copy of the photograph, an application on Form J, properly completed and signed, and a fee of $6. Deposits are not returned, so do not send your only copy.

Procedure to Follow if Work Is Later Published. If the photograph is later reproduced in copies and published, it is necessary to make a second registration, following the procedure outlined below. To maintain copyright protection, all copies of the published edition must contain a copyright notice in the required form and position.

Published photographs

What Is "Publication"? Publication, generally, means the sale, placing on sale, or public distribution of copies. Unrestricted public exhibition of a photograph may also constitute publication

How to Secure Copyright in a Published Photograph:

1. Produce copies with copyright notice.
2. Publish the work.
3. Register the copyright claim, following the instructions on page 1 of this form.

The Copyright Notice. In order to secure copyright protection in a published work, it is important that all copies contain the statutory copyright notice. The notice should appear on the photograph itself, or, if the work is a collection of photographs in book form, on the title page or verso thereof. It should ordinarily consist of the word "Copyright," the abbreviation "Copr.," or the symbol

©, accompanied by the name of the copyright owner. The year date of publication may be included in the notice, but normally it is not required unless the work could also be regarded as a "book."

—*Alternative Form of Notice.* As an alternative, the notice for photographs may consist of the symbol ©, accompanied by the initials, monogram, or mark of the copyright owner, provided the owner's name appears on some accessible part of the copies.

—*Universal Copyright Convention Notice.* Use of the symbol © with the name of the copyright owner and the year date of publication may result in securing copyright in countries which are parties to the Universal Copyright Convention. Example: © John Doe 1974.

NOTE: If copies are published without the required notice, the right to secure copyright is lost and cannot be restored.

FOR COPYRIGHT OFFICE USE ONLY	
Application received	
One copy received	
Two copies received	
Fee received	

title and interest in and to the photographs, and every part thereof, and in and to the copyright to the photographs to hold the same absolutely throughout the world for the full period of copyright, including all extensions, renewals and revisions thereof and thereafter (insofar as she is able) in perpetuity.

A logical question arises as to how a photographer can have the time, energy *and* money to register every time he shoots. Indeed a problem. Top photographers have figured out how to copyright in bulk or to protect their works in another form. For example, one photographer's method was simply to line up his best works and put them together in a collection and copyright them in a book form. That's one way of doing it. Another is to transfer a number of photographs onto one photograph and register that. What do we mean? Simple. Line up your best works on the floor and take one picture embodying all of them. Register that picture.

Also, by checking with the Copyright Office, you might find that they have an arrangement for bulk registration. And, of course, another is simply to hold a common law copyright on those photographs which are unpublished, switching to statutory registrations once the work is published.

The area which most readily follows is that of infringement and the bulk of the litigation arises in this area. In effect, it is an invasion of your work.

Supposedly, if you have secured a copyright on your photograph, you have secured protection against unauthorized uses. This also applies to copying the same work in the same medium as well as other media.

For example, a copyright in a photograph precludes the unauthorized copying of said photograph by drawing, or in any other form, as well as by photographic reproduction. A leading case of a few years ago, dealt with a photographer's picture that was later published in a magazine as a drawing. The drawing itself under the Copyright Act constituted a copyright infringement. (There was no actual decision on this case as it was settled out of court.)

There is no question but that a photographer can shoot the same scene as another photographer and even from the same spot. No one has exclusive rights to the third stone next to the second crack on Avenue Octave Gréard for a closeup shot of the Eiffel Tower.

However, the question of infringement comes into play if a photographer purposely and intentionally tries his best to copy the copyrighted shot of another photographer.

We have now stepped into an area which is the most troublesome in the whole law of copyright: Fair Use.

For instance, *Time* magazine is a copyrighted publication. Here is a photograph of former President Nixon standing at his former desk with *Time* magazine lying on the floor next to the former desk. The magazine has a drawing of President Gerald Ford on its cover.

Any infringement here? No. There is no infringement of either the copyright of the magazine or of the artist who drew the cover.

It is important to understand the two uses of a copyrighted work: permissible use (one with the permission of the copyright holder) and fair use, a use technically forbidden by the law but allowed as reasonable and customary. Those are the key words: "reasonable and customary," and they are the criteria of fair use.

Fair use is often found in the areas of editorial work and reviews, where reviewers quote certain lines or passages from a book or publish a photograph from a picture book to provide an example from the book itself.

A photographer once asked what happens with the elements in a photograph. Can they be copied?

As an example, here are certain three-dimensional objects: a square block of wood, a triangular block of wood and a round block of wood. A photograph encompassing these three objects is taken. The three objects are really uncopyrightable except as they appear in the photograph. Thus, since a copyrighted photograph of three uncopyrightable three-dimensional objects protects only the original elements of perspective, angle, etc., as contained in the copyrighted photograph, one who creates such three-dimensional objects by copying from the photograph has copied only the noncopyrightable elements of the copyrighted photograph and hence has made a noninfringing copy. Confusing? If so, add one other factor. This use may also be regarded as a form of fair use.

Now, let's take a closer look at this area of fair use and a very famous case: *Time Inc.* v. *Bernard Geis Associates* (293 F. Supp. 130 [1968]).

Abraham Zapruder of Dallas, Texas, planned to take home movies of President Kennedy's arrival in Dallas with his 8mm camera. He started the film as the caravan approached, and when the assassination occurred, he caught it all. Three copies of the film were made. Two were given to the Secret Service with a proviso that they were restricted to government use. The third, Zapruder sold to *Life* magazine. In return, he received $150,000 in installments of $25,000 a year.

Life, incidentally, gave the Warren Commission use of the film and the right to reproduce thirty frames in its report. In May of 1967, *Life* registered the film in the Copyright Office.

Bernard Geis Associates, a publisher, requested permission from *Life* to use the pictures in a book entitled "Six Seconds in Dallas" by Thomas Thompson. A royalty was to be paid; however, *Life* refused the arrangement.

Geis and Thompson reproduced the frames anyway by making charcoal sketches. The book was published and *Life* brought suit for copyright infringement.

The Court ruled that *Life* had indeed a valid copyright in the film and that sketches of same were considered copies of such film. Accordingly, a copyright infringement existed "unless the use of copyrighted material in the book is a 'fair use' outside of limits of copyright protection." The Court found in favor of Geis and Thompson, holding that the utilization of the film was indeed a fair use. It said:

> There is an initial reluctance to find any fair use by defendants because of the conduct of Thompson in making his copies and because of the deliberate appropriation in the book, in defiance of the copyright owner. Fair use presupposes good faith and fair dealing. On the other hand, it was not the nighttime activities of Thompson which enabled the defendants to reproduce copies of the Zapruder frames in the book. They could have been secured from the National Archives or they could have used the reproductions in the Warren Report or in the issues of *Life* itself. Moreover, while hope by a defendant for commercial gain is not a significant factor in this circuit, there is a strong point for defendants in their offer to surrender to *Life* all profits of Bernard Geis from the book as royalty payment for a license to use the copyrighted Zapruder frames.
>
> There is a public interest in having the fullest information available on the murder of President Kennedy. Thompson did serious work on the subject and he has a theory entitled

to public consideration. While doubtless the theory could be explained with sketches . . . the explanation actually made in the book is easier to understand. The book is not bought because it contained the Zapruder pictures; the book is bought because of the theory of Thompson and its explanation supported by the Zapruder pictures.

There seems little if any injury to Plaintiff, the copyright owner. There is no competition between plaintiff and defendants. Plaintiff does not see the pictures as such and no market for the copyrighted work appears to be affected. Defendants do not publish a magazine. There are projects for use by plaintiff of the film in the future as a motion picture or in books, but the effect of the use of certain frames in the book on such projects is speculative. It seems more reasonable to speculate that the book would, if anything, enhance the value of the copyrighted work; it is difficult to see any decrease in its value.

Ah, a question from the back row. Does fair use of a photograph apply to unpublished works at common law? The answer is no. Fair use applies only to published works.

Finally, we come to the area of damages.

In some cases, copyright statutes provide that certain minimum damages must be awarded to the copyright owner once he has proved copyright infrigement in a lawsuit. For example, should a newspaper unknowingly infringe a copyright by reproducing a copyrighted photograph, the minimum damages would be $50 with a maximum of $200. For periodicals, other than a newspaper, it's $250 and $5000 respectively. But consider this. Although these statutorily set damages may not seem to be unduly large amounts, you might want to note a particular passage from the federal copyright statute (17 U.S.C.A.) under a heading known as Damages & Profits; Amounts; Other Remedies:

To pay to the copyright proprietor such damages as the copyright proprietor may have suffered due to the infringement, as well as all the profits which the infringers shall have made from such infringement, and in proving profits the plaintiff shall be required to prove sales only, and the defendant shall be required to prove every element of cost which he claims, or in lieu of actual damages and profits, such damages as to the court shall appear just. . . .

Enough said!

Now, to bring you up to date on the latest in the fair use interpretations of the Supreme Court, you might take note of a decision just handed down by the Court dealing with the area of photocopying.

The Court has sustained as fair use the admitted practices of extensive photocopying from limited circulation medical-technical journals by the National Library of Medicine and the National Institutes of Health (*Williams & Wilkins* v. *U.S.*). The Court split 4-4 on a review of a lower court decision which had reversed an earlier victory against the two cited government libraries by the small medical book publisher.

This decision means that the lower court decision stands until either there can be new changes in the present copyright law or another case is tested.

The publisher had contended that the government library action of photocopying constituted an invasion of its legitimate market and thus was a violation of the fair use doctrine. It should be noted that the present U.S. copyright law does not provide for the massive impact of new technology, not only for copying but also for computerized and electronically stored-and-retrieved information, in any format.

What will eventually happen in this whole area of photocopying is anybody's guess. Both sides are lining up solid arguments. The ramifications of the question of photocopying are awesome and we eagerly await further legal developments in this area. However, rather than trying to figure out what may happen in the photocopying arena, let's look instead at some practical everyday questions.

1. Can photographs be copyrighted separately even if the book in which they appear is copyrighted?

Yes, because the book is copyrighted under one class and individual photographs may be copyrighted in another class. There are more than twenty classes involved, ranging from books to lectures to musical compositions to maps to drawings to motion pictures.

2. Is the use of a photograph on a book's dust jacket considered advertising?

Yes. If it is not in the public domain, it should not be used without permission. If the dust jacket has no copyright notice, then the photograph should carry a credit line.

3. Are books written under pseudonyms copyrightable under the pseudonym?

Yes.

4. Do rights, even common law rights, survive the photographer's death?

Yes.

5. How does a trademark differ from a copyright?

A trademark is an arbitrary symbol, word or phrase which is devised and used by a manufacturer or dealer to designate his goods and which is also understood by the consuming public as denoting those particular goods and distinguishing them from other commodities of a similar kind. Trademark protection is attained pursuant to the Trademark Act (known as the Lanham Act) of 1905. For example, Paramount Pictures produces and distributes motion picture films. Its trademark is the mountain, clouds, stars and the word "Paramount" scripted across. That logo, or symbol, represents its product and means that Paramount has an exclusive right to utilize that logo on its goods in a particular channel of trade. Trademark registration is under the jurisdiction of the Commissioner of Patents and that office issues a simplified booklet of instructions for those interested in securing trademark registration of a particular logo, symbol, word, phrase, etc.

TO SUMMARIZE

Immediately upon the film being processed, make sure the copyright legend, as suggested in this section, is placed on the back of every black-and-white negative and on the face of every transparency. Every print too should have the legend. This way you will prevent any dedication to the public (i.e., public domain) and you will have served notice to the world.

If you are acquiring a copyright in a work previously copyrighted, then follow the suggestions outlined in this section on assignments.

And finally, to close this rather laborious and serious subject, let's turn to something a bit more humorous. Humorous but true.

A book was brought out recently. It was filled with 192 blank pages and was aptly called *The Nothing Book*. It sold for $3.00.

We hear that the publishers of this book might be sued for copyright infringement. Apparently, in 1972, a book was published in Belgium entitled *Memoirs of an Amnesiac*. It also consisted of empty pages.

The *Memoirs* author, so the reports say, is suing for plagiarism. The *Nothing Book* people don't seem too concerned though. According to newspaper reports, the *Nothing Book* "editor" doesn't take the suit too seriously. She says that the idea was that of her publisher who never saw the *Memoirs* before and besides, she says, you can't copyright an idea (which you can't). Not deterred, last December, the *Nothing Book* people brought out a new deluxe edition in a marble design hand binding selling for $5.00.

We understand it sold quite well.

6

Is My Picture Obscene?

A poem dating from 1926 called "She Being Brand" by e.e. cummings concerns what appears to be on one level the breaking in of a car, while on a deeper level it is about a man's attempt to seduce a girl, a virgin at that. What the poet seems to be doing is offering the reader a detailed explanation of the foreplay involved. It's quite provocative, to say the least, and to this day—over fifty years later—we have seen many a young damsel blush reading this particular poem. Not because of the language, mind you. There is not a single obscene word. But it's just the way the poet strung the words together that gave it a provocative effect. Obscene? Obscenity could easily be said to be in the mind's eye. But, that's only one aspect of this field of obscenity.

Try this on for size.

Penthouse magazine, more specifically, its November, 1974, issue, had a cover photo which wound up in court. The November, 1974, issue had on its cover a partly nude woman—nothing that extraordinary for *Penthouse*.

The woman faced the camera. She was in a semi-reclining position, one of her breasts fully exposed, the other partly so. Her genital area was covered.

The New York City Police Department ordered a number of newsstands in New York City to remove the full cover displays of this particular issue of *Penthouse*. If they didn't, they faced arrest for displaying offensive sexual materials. What do you think happened? Well, before we go into the court's decision, let's take a look at where obscenity has been and where it might be going.

Obscenity is a strange field. Strange because it has yet to be understood. The recent enactments of various legislative bodies around the country and the latest court decisions have shown a remarkable ability to create sheer chaos out of what was once simple disorder.

It is no secret that more and more of the courts' time is being taken up by suits involving alleged pornographic books, magazines and movies. The problem is that nobody is sure of what pornographic really means. In fact, back in 1948, Justice Robert H. Jackson voiced the fear that the Supreme Court of the United States would eventually become the High Court of Obscenity. He may not have been too far wrong. However, we do not intend to backtrack and go through every case to illustrate what has happened in this area of the law over the years —centuries actually. Suffice it to say, it is rather perverse. But let us discuss a few key facts.

First of all, notwithstanding the First and Fourteenth amendments of the Constitution, there *are* obscenity statutes. These statutes, though, are not the only weapons the government has against allegedly obscene literature or material. One of the most important methods of suppression has been administrative censorship: the customs power and the Post Office's control of the mails.

Court battles in the obscenity area originally started because certain publications were declared nonmailable or nonimportable on grounds of what was termed "obscenity." These contests have played major roles in attempts to judicially define what is and what is not "obscene." Additionally, state statutes and local ordinances forbidding the sale or possession of obscene literature or materials have also generated many court actions which have added to judge-made laws on obscenity.

As we said before, we don't want to spend time in going back over the landmark decisions which stretch from *Fanny Hill* to *Ulysses* to Ralph Ginzburg to *Esquire* magazine to *God's Little Acre* to *Deep Throat*. The changes over the years are incredibly confusing.

But let's take a look at where the matter *now* stands.

The key case is that of *Miller* v. *the State of California* which was decided by a 5-4 split of the Supreme Court on June 21, 1973 (93 S. Ct. 2607).

A chap named Marvin Miller sent five brochures to a restaurant in Newport Beach, California. They were unsolicited. The envelope was opened by the restaurant's manager, with his mother looking on no less, and immediately they complained to the police. What was inside? Well, the brochures advertised four books: *Intercourse, Man-Woman, Sex Orgies Illustrated* and *An Illustrated History of Pornography*. Also included was a film entitled *Marital Intercourse*. The brochures were pictures of men and women in a variety of sexual positions, with their genitals displayed. After a jury trial, Miller was convicted of a misdemeanor under the California Penal Code.

The case went up to the Supreme Court of the United States. Writing for the majority, Chief Justice Burger ruled that California could punish for such conduct. He said that this case involved a "situation in which sexually explicit materials have been thrust by aggressive sales action upon unwilling recipients who had in no way indicated any desire to receive such materials."

He went on to say:

This Court has recognized that the States have a legitimate interest in prohibiting dissemination of obscene material when the mode of dissemination carries with it a significant danger of offending the sensibilities of unwilling recipients or of exposure to juveniles. . . .

It is in this context that we are called on to define the standards which must be used to identify obscene material that a State may regulate without infringing on the First Amendment as applicable to the States through the Fourteenth Amendment.

Justice Burger was attempting to formulate a new standard for obscenity. He said that the Court had been unable to muster a majority to agree on what constitutes "obscene, pornographic material" to be regulated under the individual states' police power. But he felt that in this particular matter, the Supreme Court could formulate standards more concrete than in the past. Accordingly, he wrote:

It is neither realistic nor constitutionally sound to read the First Amendment as requiring that the people of Maine or

Mississippi accept public depiction of conduct found tolerable in Las Vegas or New York City. People in different States vary in their tastes and attitudes, and this diversity is not to be strangled by the absolutism of imposed uniformity. We hold the requirement that the jury evaluating the materials with reference to "contemporary standards of the State of California" serves this protective purpose and is constitutionally adequate.

Therefore, what we have is a decision which holds that obscenity is to be determined by applying contemporary community standards, not national standards.

It should be noted that as of this writing, the Supreme Court has agreed to decide whether California's obscenity law conforms to the standards it established in 1973. The Supreme Court will consider the issue in a case involving seizure by Buena Vista police of the film *Deep Throat* when it was being shown in November, 1973. A three-judge federal court in Los Angeles had found the state law unconstitutional and California appealed. More chaos.

The Court has tried to sort out this ever-mounting problem with two highly important decisions in 1974 and 1975. In 1974 came the matter of *Jenkins* v. the *State of Georgia* (94 S. Ct. 2750). Jenkins had been convicted in Georgia for showing the film *Carnal Knowledge* in a motion picture theater.

However, the Supreme Court ruled that the film, which included scenes where sexual conduct (like "ultimate sexual acts") was understood to be taking place and which included occasional scenes of nudity, even though the camera did not focus on the actors' bodies or parts, was not obscene under currently operative constitutional standards. The Court found that the Federal Constitution did not require that juries in state obscenity actions be instructed to apply standards of a "hypothetical statewide community." In other words, such instructions may be given but their use was not mandated. Accordingly, the Court's own view of the film enabled it to reach the conclusion that the film's expression of sexual conduct was not offensive.

The ". . . showing of the film . . . is simply not the 'public portrayal of hard core sexual conduct for its own sake, and for ensuing commercial gain' which we said was punishable in Miller."

If that doesn't tangle things up a bit more, consider this latest decision, handed down on June 23, 1975, *Erznoznik* v. *City of Jacksonville* (95 S. Ct. 2268). In this matter, a Jacksonville, Florida, ordinance made it a public nuisance as well as a punishable offense for a drive-in movie theater to show films containing nudity, especially where the screen was visible from a public street. You see, Erznoznik had a drive-in theater and he was charged with violating that ordinance by showing the movie *Class of '74* which had been rated "R" by the Motion Picture Association of America. An "R" rating means that young people could not be admitted without being accompanied by a parent or guardian.

Class of '74 showed female buttocks and bare breasts and these could easily be seen from the public streets. The Court held that although each case ultimately must depend on its own specific facts, it did say that when the government, acting as censor, undertakes selectively to shield the public from some kinds of speech on the ground that they are more offensive than others, the First Amendment strictly limits its power.

The Court went on to say that the Jacksonville ordinance discriminates among movies solely on the basis of content and that its effect is to deter drive-in theaters from showing movies containing any nudity, however innocent or educational.

> This discrimination cannot be justified as a means of preventing significant intrusions on privacy. The ordinance seeks only to keep these films from being seen from public streets and places where the offended viewer readily can avert his eyes. . . . Thus, we conclude that the limited privacy interest of persons on the public streets cannot justify this censorship or otherwise protected speech on the basis of its content.

In effect, the ordinance was too broad and although the Court did not intend to demean the interests of Jacksonville, it certainly would not allow the First Amendment freedoms to be obviated.

Mr. Justice White, in his dissenting opinion, laid open the matter even more. He said:

> The Court asserts that the State may shield the public from selected types of speech and allegedly expressive conduct, such as nudity, only when the speaker or actor invades the privacy of the home or where the degree of captivity of an unwilling listener is such that it is impractical for him to avoid the exposure by averting his eyes.

The Court concludes: "That the limited privacy interest of persons on the public streets cannot justify this censorship of otherwise protected speech on the basis of its content." If this broadside is to be taken literally, the State may not forbid "expressive" nudity on the public streets, in the public parks or any other public place since other persons in those places at that time have a "limited privacy interest" and may merely look the other way.

As of now, there is great confusion about what the phrase "community standards" (as it came down from the Miller case) means. Many questions arise. Will any jury ever accurately reflect state standards? Are there really any state (or even local) standards? Is North Carolina like South Carolina? Would West Virginia agree with Virginia? Would Albany, New York, have the same values as New York City? Would Altoona, Pennsylvania, see things the same way as State College, only forty miles away?

And anyway, what is a community? Would Kentucky have 120 community standards, because it has 120 counties? This is where the situation stands, or lies, today. The same legal entanglements which closed *Deep Throat* in New York City might be used to censor Fielding's *Tom Jones* in Omaha or Hermann Hesse's *Narcissus and Goldmund* in Key Biscayne.

Now, let's go back to our friends at *Penthouse*. You remember that the New York City Police Department ordered the removal from display of the November, 1974, issue? Under the applicable New York Penal Law (Section 245.11), a person is guilty of public display of offensive sexual material when with knowledge of its content, he displays same in a manner easily visible from a public thoroughfare and which predominantly appeals to prurient interests. This, apparently, was the legislature's intent when it enacted this statute.

The court immediately noted the key words, "predominantly appeals to prurient interest in sex," and in that regard it did not find the *Penthouse* cover falling within those guidelines. It relied on a holding in another matter where the manager of a Times Square theater was convicted of having displayed publicly a film advertisement consisting of an almost life-size photograph of a nude woman in a prone position with her buttocks exposed, along with several smaller photographs that included depictions of women, some of them with breasts exposed. That conviction was overturned by the New York Court of Appeals (*People* v. *Lou Bern Broadway*, 32 NY 2d, 816 [1973]), on the basis that "the displays . . . as a matter of law, do not fall within the proscription of the statute."

Accordingly, in the *Penthouse* matter, the court held that "certainly a single eight-and-a-half by eleven-inch photograph of a woman with exposed breasts is no more offensive than the collection of displays which included a life-size depiction of naked women in prone positions and smaller photographs in which portions of women's breasts were exposed as in the [above] case" (*Penthouse International* v. *Police Commissioner Codd,* as reported in the *New York Law Journal* of November 19, 1974—Supreme Court, State of New York).

Enough said!

How about the Post Office? How does it fit in, especially with respect to the mailing of certain questionable materials? In 1968, an antipandering statute went into effect (39 U.S. Code, 4009). It said, in part:

Whoever for himself, or by his agents or assigns, mails or causes to be mailed any pandering advertisement which offers for sale matter which the addressee in his sole discretion believes to be erotically arousing or sexually provocative shall be subject to an order of the Postmaster General to refrain from further mailings of such materials to designated addresses. . . .

The wording of this statute places considerable discretion in the hands of the recipient of the materials. If a person receives mail which offends him, he can complain to his Post Office. If the recipient requests that no more materials be sent to him by a specific sender, the Post Office Department can order the sender to discontinue all mailings to the recipient. Also, the Postmaster General can order that the recipient's name be removed from all mailing lists of the sender. If the mailings continue, another complaint from the recipient can result in the Post Office Department's requesting the Justice Department to get a court order to halt such mailings.

The motion picture area bears reexamination here especially since much in the way of court decisions seems to be coming via that route. It should be noted that the *Miller* v. *California* situation now throws the issue back a few years to when local censorship could and would prevent almost any motion picture from being shown.

In order to sidestep such local censorship, the Motion Picture

Association of America established, a number of years ago, a Production Code and Rating Administration and rated films according to the "G," "GP," "R" and "X" classifications. However, this rating system does not prevent the banning of a picture pursuant to the Miller decision.

TO SUMMARIZE

The problems of defining and controlling obscenity—whether in the electronic or print media or in motion pictures—are among the most tangled in all of American law.

The thrust of the fury is really against vendors and distributors. It is not the taking of the photograph which is of the prime importance; it is the distribution of same.

What is obscenity again? Well, as Justice Potter Stewart of the Supreme Court has noted, the Court persists in "trying to define what may be indefinable."

Book Publishing: What Do I Do?

When the word "publishing" is mentioned, the photographer quickly thinks of a magazine publishing a photograph of his; a newspaper doing likewise; an order by a customer of copies of a dog photo for submission in a contest. Most photographers realize that there is some kind of market for their photographs: magazine and newspaper reproductions, advertising and promotional uses, record album covers, and other uses falling under the term "publishing."

The careful photographer, staying within the guidelines set up in the previous chapters, can pretty much publish what he takes. But, it is interesting to note that most photographers are not fully aware of the many publishing avenues which are open to them besides the ones mentioned above. They may know fully the ins and outs of photojournalism, or about the advertising market or about taking someone's portrait or even doing a bar mitzvah or a wedding. But there is one particular area which most photographers completely overlook: it is books. And it is this market which by and large affords the photographer one of his greatest satisfactions. After all, he can have a book published—a real book—set in type, with beautiful plates, bound with a fancy cover, with the photographer's name ace high on the cover, on the spine, on the front page. He can watch it go into print. He can watch it being distributed across the country. He can look at the press releases, save the reviews (especially if they are glowing) and then, to top it off, he can walk by Doubleday's on Fifth Avenue or Kroch's and Brentano's in Chicago, Pickwick's in Los Angeles, the Harvard Coop in Boston or Rich's in Atlanta—not to mention the countless other stores and places throughout the country and the world— and he can see his name in the front window or on a shelf or on a display table. Instant immortality. We are not being sarcastic. That's pretty heavy stuff to overlook.

There is no doubt that the publishing industry affords the photographer quite an avenue on which to tread. But, in this field of book publishing, the photographer is most ignorant and he shouldn't be.

Contrary to what you may have been reading in newspapers and magazines, book sales have not dropped off. In fact, during the past ten years, they have doubled. That's right. It is estimated that sales reached $3 billion last year. Actually, over 40,000 new titles were published.

It must be understood that not every book can become a best seller. And it may not matter either. Some non-best sellers do very well indeed. But, aside from the best sellers, most publishers make their money from such items as textbooks, special reference works, dictionaries and other reference books, books on diet, sex manuals, how-to manuals, and subsidiary rights.

Subsidiary rights? To fully explain the importance of what is probably for most photographers an unfamiliar term, let's take a closer look at the book publishing industry itself.

Where is the break-even point for a book? Each publisher computes it differently. Generally, if a book sells between 8,000 to 10,000 copies, the publisher will be making money, unless, of course, his costs are usually large. In this connection, there are many people in publishing who claim that rising production costs in the publishing industry have sent everything soaring. That's quite true. In fact, in the last ten years, many have more than doubled. When that happens the retail price of the book must rise. But even that gets out of hand. Twenty-five years ago, the average book sold for under $5. Today, the publishers are attempting to keep it under $10. And good photography books, well, they can run from $15 on up—and up. Where are books sold? Good question.

In the United States alone, there are approximately 130,000 outlets. A small percentage of these are the good old-fashioned bookstores. The estimate is around 2,500. The other places where books are sold are in libraries, in tobacco shops, pharmacies, card stores, supermarkets, department stores, transportation centers. What are the publishing houses today? Who are they? As recently as twenty years ago, most of the publishing houses were privately owned. Today, companies in private hands are becoming the exception to the rule. CBS owns Holt Rinehart and Winston; RCA owns Random House which in turn owns Knopf; ITT owns Bobbs-Merrill; Gulf & Western (which owns Paramount Pictures) now owns Simon & Schuster which also owns Pocket Books; Litton Industries owns American Book.

With these rather drastic changes, it would seem that book publishing has an appeal to industry. It remains a good source of supply for other areas. Does Gulf & Western not expect to pick up some good works from Simon & Schuster for its Paramount Pictures subsidiary? Does CBS really think that it can't benefit from some of the Holt Rinehart product?

What we are dealing with is what we mentioned before: subsidiary rights. Indeed, we have heard it said from more than one source that in the book publishing business subsidiary rights are the tail wagging the dog.

What are subsidiary rights? How do they apply? They are the allied rights which generally flow from the publication of a book. Examples are: paperback rights, magazine rights, serial rights, motion pictures, television, stage, etc. They can be most lucrative for a publisher. Works of fiction especially will afford a company much additional revenue in the way of subsidiary rights. But, how does that affect you, the photographer? Who's going to make a movie out of a picture book?

You'd be surprised. One book we know of was optioned for a television special. It was a work by a well-known imaginative photographer working in black and white, whose subject and theme were the dreams of children. Another book involved the photographs of a particular horse, a record-breaker. The interest here was for a documentary film. There was also another interest in fictionalizing the horse and the episodes of its life in making a feature-length motion picture.

Still another book dealing with the Bicentennial was bought by a publishing house. The contract provided for the utilization of the work in connection with a series of television specials on the country's 200th birthday. The advance to the photographer was $40,000 and he still has a good share of the royalties.

What is a publisher looking for? Well, almost anything goes. Some publishers will print anything that comes down the pike; some specialize in certain areas; some will print picture books only if there is a full text alongside to supplement the photographs.

As we said before, most publishers want what the public will want. This indicates something with a "hook" to it, a book of pictures which have a theme, a viewpoint, a stance—with or without a text. Too often, a photographer takes pictures at random of people, subway trains, farmlands, but with no real connection. In other words, pictures which say very little as a group. Then, he wonders why no publisher wants to spend the time and energy and money in printing his pictures.

It is not a cheap proposition to publish picture books. The cost of plates, the composition, paper, etc., is quite high and the publisher is not going to be interested in satisfying a whim —not if he wants to stay in business. After all, he must still show a profit for whatever he prints.

Therefore it is important for the photographer to find that hook, to give the publisher something of substance, imagination, interest, something that will make him want to spend his money in printing the photographer's work. Once you have this "something," you must get it to a publisher.

The way to shop an idea is rather simple. It is as easy as what a writer does. Take the pictures you want incorporated in a book, put them in some kind of binder or folder, with an explanation of what direction you want the book to take or what the book is about (or if there is text, include that), and take it to the publisher. The worst they can say is no, and they might just say yes. When you get to that point, you will obviously be given an offer: "We would like to publish this picture book on the marriage ritual of the tetse fly of Africa."

When you pick yourself up from the floor, you will hear a few kind remarks from the publisher, usually explaining how little an advance they can pay and that you will be receiving their standard form contract. Then, there will be thrust in front of you a contract four pages long, containing some twenty different provisions, neatly numbered and including some of the teeniest print imaginable.

"This is our standard form. We have filled in your name on the top line and the name of the book. Just sign there on page four."

If you have been too caught up with seeing your name on a contract and haven't had the time or the inclination to review the twenty-odd provisions, then you may, for the most part, be in for a rude awakening when the time comes for the payment of royalties . . . not to mention the actual way the book is published.

We are not saying publishers are cheaters. We are not saying they are sidewinding thieves. They are business people who are offering you a contract, and some may offer a contract which is most favorable to their side. And the photographer (no matter how hungry he may be) must watch the contract provisions carefully or he may find that he has either undersold himself and his work, or worse yet, he has given away something which he really had no intention whatsoever of giving away. Now, the publisher doesn't know this. Remember, the publisher will not protect the photographer. The photographer must protect himself and more often than not, he must protect himself from himself.

Enough of the scare tactics. Back to the contract.

Most contracts offered to photographers by most publishing houses are not really applicable to photographers. They are writers' contracts and, therefore, many of the provisions contained in them are not relevant to photographs.

The photographer, of course, can always draft his own contract, if he wishes, but generally publishers will offer their contracts and make the reasonable changes you desire.

Most publishers are reputable and if your suggestions are realistic, there is really no problem in obtaining the necessary changes. The problem is in understanding what changes are necessary.

There is a sample photographer's book contract currently in use. It is contained in the ASMP *Guide to Business Practices.* Admittedly, this contract is merely a guide, but it will give you at least a jumping-off spot.

Now, let's look at a typical publisher's contract.

The opening paragraphs usually concern what grant of rights is being given by the photographer. If you signed the contract as is, you would generally find that you had given away worldwide, all-language, exclusive rights for publication of your photographs in book form.

First of all, ask yourself what it is that you want to grant. Do you want the publisher to have worldwide rights, in any country, or do you want him to have American rights only?

Also, when we talk about the term, the publisher will want a full term of copyright plus any extensions and renewals thereof. As you may remember from the chapter on copyright, the United States is still working with the two 28-year terms. We have found it eminently fair for the publisher to receive only the first (28-year) term of the U.S. copyright. That should more than cover their use of the photographs in the particular book.

The next thing to consider is delivery of the photographs. When are they to be delivered? How are they to be delivered? What is to be delivered? The ramifications here are considerably more than with a manuscript. First of all, you, the photographer, may be submitting original color transparencies or black-and-white negatives to the publisher from which plates are to be made.

That being so, somebody had better take the responsibility of looking after those original materials. This should be the publisher's domain. Once those materials leave your hands, they should become the responsibility of the publisher and must be returned to you in the same condition in which they were sent. In this connection, the publisher should agree to an insurer's liability for such materials so that in the event they are lost or damaged, then you would be compensated for them.

The clause which is now being used is the same contained in invoices and delivery memos. This is described in more detail in Chapter 8.

There must also be some sort of provision concerning the time the materials come back to you. Certainly, after the plates are made and found satisfactory is not unreasonable. Within thirty days after the publication of the book is even less unreasonable.

Much of the language in publishing contracts relates to the delivery and acceptance of a satisfactory manuscript, which is really of no moment to the photographer.

If there are any special provisions on the kind of photographs to be submitted, or in what form, or how many, etc., then that should be spelled out in the contract.

Warranties and indemnities are potentially more trouble than most photographers care to realize. The publisher obviously, and with perfect right, wants the photographer to warrant that (a) the photographs are free and clear, (b) they are not in the public domain and (c) they are not obscene, lewd, or violate any right of any other party.

All of these phrases could be toned down somewhat.

The photographer can only make warranties to the best of his knowledge; in other words, to the best of his knowledge, the photographer has the right to grant the rights under the contract to the publisher.

Insofar as his holding the publisher harmless in case of any action against him, this is a two-way street. The publisher must similarly indemnify the photographer against any actions arising from matters inserted in the book without the photographer's approval. The photographer cannot be left holding the bag for any and every legal action. Some photographers with considerable clout have been able to have written into their contracts language to the effect that the publisher will also indemnify them from certain libel and privacy suits in instances where the publisher could have determined immediately that there was danger in printing certain materials.

As we noted in the copyright section, there is sometimes a question on who holds the copyright in the book. Although the publication contract will often say that the publisher will copyright the book, it must be spelled out that the copyright is always to be in the name of the photographer. There are very few publishing houses that will not consent to this, but the photographer should be aware, nevertheless, that it is important for him to be the copyright owner of his work. In effect, then, the publisher is simply picking up a license to publish what the photographer owns.

This is the way it should be. If there is text involved in a particular book, then it is quite proper to have two copyright notices and registrations involved: one for the text and one for the photographs.

If the photographer decides to give the publisher both the original term of copyright plus the renewal as the period of license, the photographer must never rely on his publisher to renew the copyright. After all, 28 years later, the publisher may have forgotten the book or returned the rights to the photographer or even gone out of business. While the usual clause provides that the publisher will renew the work when the time comes, the photographer must make sure that the renewal application is filed, or if necessary, file it himself.

At this point, the contract will probably go on to talk about revisions and corrections and proofs, etc. Most of these clauses are really not applicable to the photographer. The one point the photographer should consider is with respect to the layout itself. Does the photographer have any right to approve the layout? What about the cropping of pictures? What about the title and the captions? Whatever approval the photographer feels he should have must be spelled out in the contract; otherwise, the photographer really has no legal recourse if something goes wrong.

We now come to what the photographer may consider the guts of the contract: money. Here is where understanding is needed, not only of the terms used but of what royalties the photographer may earn. For instance, some publishing houses pay very little in the way of an advance but do give decent royalties. This means, in effect, that they are gambling on the book sales being good so that they and the photographer will make some money. This is something the photographer has to weigh carefully. If he feels he has a hot item, then he may wish to forego a larger advance and take his chances on the sale of the book. If, on the other hand, he feels there is little market for the book, then the photographer may wish to take a larger advance . . . also known as "take the money and run."

Advances differ considerably. They can range anywhere from $1,500 to $50,000. Some may even be higher and some lower. The thing to remember generally about advances is that they apply *against* the royalty payment. This means that if the photographer receives a hefty advance, that money will have to be recouped by the publisher before royalty payments are made.

Most advances should be made on a nonreturnable basis; that is, if the publisher later on decides not to publish the book or defaults in any way, the photographer does not have to return the advance. It also works the other way: The publisher is well within his rights to ask for the return of the advance if the photographer does not perform. Of course, there is the question of what the "photographer not performing" means.

The area of royalties may cause a problem for both the photographer and the publisher. The publisher generally tries to keep payments modest to prevent book prices from going up too much. The photographer, on the other hand, wants to make sure he is not being taken advantage of. In this area, there is a great deal of give-and-take.

For example, many contracts provide for royalties on a sliding scale. This means, a given percentage on the first so many thousand copies sold, then a higher percentage on the next so many copies sold, etc. The problem is to figure out what percentages apply to what quantities and the basis for determining sales.

Each publisher may work differently. For the most part, it is difficult to try to standardize percentages, since much depends on the product to be sold; however, the photographer might want to consider the following arrangement: A minimum of 10% on the first 5,000 copies sold; then an increase to 12½% on the next 5,000 copies sold; and on all copies in excess of those 10,000, a 15% royalty. Of course, certain established people obtain better terms, and there are often reasons for less favorable terms.

Now, there must be thought given to the price on which the royalty is to be calculated. Some publishers gear it to the retail price of the books. Some work with net (wholesale) prices. Some with suggested list, etc. The Authors Guild of America recommends that the percentage be determined by the suggested retail list price of the book. Here is what the Guild says about this approach: "The publisher alone determines his selected list price, and thus the dollar amount of the author's royalty. The list price could be $8 or $2. But at $2, a 10% royalty would be only 20 cents, not 80 cents. This clause does not prevent the publisher from setting his list price as low as he wishes. But if the minimum amount inserted is $6.00 (for example) and the publisher reduces his list price to $5.00, he must nevertheless compute royalties on the basis of $6." There are, of course, other variables and other avenues to consider, such as establishing a floor below which the royalty rate could not be reduced by quantity discounts and the basis for discounts.

These are points that the photographer must carefully consider, especially if he is going to negotiate his own contract. He must be able to read every word in the contract and understand what it means; otherwise, he may find that he doesn't get his share of the pie until and upon the happening of certain events, many of which the photographer would never have agreed to if he knew what they meant.

There are many, many aspects of royalty payments and much really depends on what you, the photographer, have agreed to give the publisher. Rights take many forms, from book club licenses to paperback licenses to abridgments to foreign rights to serial rights to filmstrips to computers to stage, motion pictures and on and on.

It is important to understand and consider what you are giving the publisher and then to specify the income from those items. Whatever is not to be a part of the deal obviously must be stricken from the contract.

It is not possible to analyze every detail of a publishing contract here. There are too many variations, but the photographer should be aware of certain guidelines to follow. As further examples, the publisher may want soft-cover or paperback rights included. The income provisions take different forms here. If the publisher wishes to print his own paperback edition, then the sums paid to the photographer differ from the leasing of paperback rights by the publishers to a paperback firm. In the former case, it is not unusual for the photographer to receive a royalty of 6% up to 10,000 copies and an 8% royalty on copies over that quantity. If the publisher is interested in granting such rights to another firm, then the royalty rate is different. In such an event, the photographer might try to get 50% of the first $10,000 of income received by the publisher, 60% on the next $10,000 and 70% above $20,000 although traditionally this income is split fifty-fifty. Naturally, this should be based on all monies received by the publisher without deductions of any kind. It would also be a good idea for the photographer to consider obtaining approval of the disposition of paperback rights. There are some books that lend themselves to the paperback market better than the hard-cover market and it may just be that the photographer might be able to make a better deal in this respect. That being so, the photographer should at least have the right to bring a deal to the publisher or to better a proposed deal. Of course, this is all a throwback to what you the photographer are granting to the publisher.

Filmstrips, motion pictures, television and similar rights present quite another problem. If you are dealing with a relatively small advance or you wish to retain certain rights other than the publication of the book, then you had best watch yourself carefully in this area. The filmstrip, motion picture, television and merchandising markets are booming. As we will discuss in Chapter 12, markets for photographers' work have opened up considerably and if there are certain areas you want protected, then you had better spell them out quite clearly in your contract. Some publishers will demand exclusive rights; some will work jointly with the photographer; in some cases, the photographer will reserve all these rights and retain all the income.

In many instances authors of certain nonfiction books who conceded a large share of certain rights to the publisher on the theory that the rights would never sell, lived to regret it.

In any event, the one aspect which must constantly be kept in the forefront of your mind is that you are basically granting the publisher the right to print certain of your work in a book. If it is not your intention to have the publisher take your photographs from that book and market them separately (e.g., postcards, posters, calendars), then you must make sure you are protected by the wording of the contract. This same principle may also apply to similars, dupes or rejected photographs. Do you want to have the right to utilize those? We can understand the publishers' viewpoint and they would be perfectly within their rights to ask you to refrain from coming out with a similar product during the time they are trying to sell your book. No problem here. And by the same token, you would like to know when the publisher intends to publish. So, try to insert a stipulation that obligates the publisher to publish the book within a certain time, say one year after delivery of the completed manuscript.

Once we deal with money, we have to move into accounting. Generally, a publisher will render statements and pay royalties on a semiannual basis. Although the Authors Guild recommends quarterly accountings, each publisher varies in the way it keeps its books. In any event, you want your statement and your money (if any) as soon as possible after the close of the accounting period. The longer the publisher holds the money, the more interest you lose. Generally ninety days is this rule, but you might try for thirty to sixty days after the close of the period.

Also, you should have the right to audit the publisher's books and records and, in that respect, if you find an error amounting to more than 5%, then the publisher should be responsible for paying for that audit.

Most publishers want to withhold a certain sum to cover returns. This is known as a reserve. The publishing industry is one of the few areas where unrestricted returns are permitted. This means that books really go out to the booksellers on a kind of consignment basis, and if the books don't sell, the bookseller has the right to return them to the publisher. The publisher tries to protect himself by withholding a certain percentage of the monies due the photographer to cover these returned books so that the publisher is not placed in a position of overpaying the photographer. In this connection, a reserve of not more than 15% of the royalties which would otherwise be paid would generally be in line with common practice today.

The other provisions in the "standard" contract are relatively minor, compared with those we have discussed. But the photographer should not overlook anything.

For example, the photographer should be given at least ten free copies of the work upon its publication with the right to order more copies at a discount of 40%. A book is to be deemed out of print when copies are not available through regular trade channels and are not listed in the publisher's catalog. What this means is that the rights would revert to the photographer in such event or at least he has the right to purchase the plates back for a certain reduced sum. The reason for this is that the publisher just may be unsuccessful in doing something with the book and the photographer may just feel he can do something better with it. He should not have to wait until the actual rights expire, especially if they run for the term of the copyright (and possibly renewal). There are other interesting paragraphs such as suits for infringement. What happens when there is a suit against another party for infringement? It's happened many, many times. The contract must spell out who shares in the costs and who shares in the recovery.

Finally, there are two specific clauses which, for the most part, may be unacceptable.

One deals with the option and the other with deductions. The option clause gives the publisher the privilege of publishing the photographer's next book, if the publisher chooses to do so. This is a one-way street. If a photographer is satisfied with what the publisher has done with his first book, obviously he will come back. The second unacceptable clause deals with the right of the publisher to deduct from this particular contract certain monies that may be owed him under another contract. Unless this is carefully spelled out, it could lead to abuse. The only justification is that returns might be heavy, causing an overpayment that could never be recouped. In any event each publishing contract should be treated as a separate venture. In other words, each contract should stand on its own. The photographer should receive his money when he is supposed to and there should be no withholding or deduction of same for any reason.

This, now, is the bulk of what the photographer should look for in his contact with the publisher. There are a myriad of other elements involved, but these are all subject to negotiation, depending on the book to be published, the publisher and the photographer.

TO SUMMARIZE

Photographers can publish what they like provided they have followed the legal requirements as set forth in this chapter and others in this book.

The book publishing industry is an extremely good outlet for photographers; however, their dealings with publishers require a close knowledge of the field, the product involved, how it is produced and distributed, and the agreements among the parties.

8

Losses, Damages, Holding: Can I Collect?

What happens when photographs go out of your shop? Well, for one thing, they can be lost. They can also be damaged. They can be retained for too long a period. They can be used without your consent.

Most photographers and most users of photography have been completely ignorant of what value photographs and transparencies have and what rights the parties have as to liability.

Take, for example, a transparency. Is it really valuable? To say so would be a gross understatement. It is the only original fruit left of the photographer's labors. If it is lost, there is nothing. The transparency, like the negative for a black and white, is the original work coming out of the camera. Most users of photography demand to see such original work to determine if it can be used. Duplicates are not asked for because such users of photography know that duplicates are second-generation work and do not accurately reflect what the finished product will look like. Therefore, so long as original work must be utilized, the photographer must learn to protect himself. And the user must be able to recognize the liability he can be exposed to.

Each photograph stands on its own. It is immaterial whether it is part of a sequence or not. A photograph is an accounting of a specific time and place. How, then, do we determine the liability of a user of photography? The first and foremost rule is for the photographer *never* to send something out of his shop without proper papers attached to it. We have already discussed the copyright notice which must go on every photograph (and when we use the word "photograph," we are talking about transparencies and negatives too).

Now, we must turn to the actual piece of paper which protects the photograph on its travels.

A contract or some sort of confirmation will, by and large and if worded properly, offer the greatest measure of protection. The law backs this up. Under the Uniform Commercial Code, Section 2-201, a writing in confirmation of a contract which is neither rejected nor objected to, within ten days, by the receiving party is enforceable. Naturally, this does not mean that you can willy-nilly send people contracts and expect to bind them in the event they don't answer within ten days. But note specifically the key words, "a writing in confirmation of a contract."

Let's take a specific example.

A photographer is requested to send to the customer a number of transparencies of birds. This he does along with a contract or some sort of paper evidencing that he is sending the customer a certain number of transparencies at the customer's request. The customer will be held liable for those transparencies since he has had an opportunity to reject the piece of paper and the transparencies (if there was something he didn't like about the deal) but chose instead to hold on to them.

There are numerous cases backing up this principle. In New York, for example, *Soundview Woods* v. *Town of Mamaroneck* (178 NYS 2d, 800 [1958]) holds that in the absence of a statute requiring a signature, parties may become bound by the terms of a contract even though they do not sign it, where their assent is otherwise indicated.

In fact, it is not even necessary that both parties sign a contract to make it an agreement in writing.

There are some—many—who will say that the mere physical acceptance of a contract unilateral in form does not make the recipient a party to a contract so as to bind him to its performance. This is true, but it should be noted that a party by receiving and retaining, without objection, a contact may, under certain circumstances, be held bound by its terms though he himself has not signed it. The case of *Newburger* v. *American Surety Co.* (242 NY 134 [1926]) shows that if a person has accepted a written agreement and has acted upon it, he may be bound by it although he has not signed it. Additionally, the entire agreement may be enforced if a party accepts and receives the goods of another or makes partial payment (*Helen Whiting, Inc.* v. *Trojan Textile Corp.*, 307 NY 360 [1954]). There are even further examples to establish the binding agreement: In *Stove* v. *Ransel Trading Corp.* (190 NYS 2d 84 [1958]), it was held that an agreement may be oral although there is a written note or memorandum of its terms. In a leading U.S. case, *General Talking Pictures Corp.* v. *Western Electric Co.* (59 S. Ct. 116 [1939]), it was established that if the terms of an agreement are plainly stamped on a machine, a contract between the buyer and the seller to observe those terms may arise, when the buyer accepts delivery of the machine. This case involved a motion picture projector where the terms and conditions of use were stamped on the machine instead of by way of a separate piece of paper.

Other cases also stand in back of this concept. In New York, there is *Stein, Hall & Co.* v. *Nestle-Le Mur Co.* (13 Misc 2d 547 [1958]). Another one of similar magnitude is *Exeter Mfg. Co.* v. *Marrus* (5 NYS 2d 438 [1938]), providing that a party by receiving and retaining an agreement by another party may be bound by the terms thereof although his signature does not appear thereon. This is also the view in *Japan Cotton Trading Co.* v. *Farber* (253 NYS 290 [1931]).

In case you're wondering, other jurisdictions have similar findings: *Brandt* v. *Beebe* (332 SW 2d 463—a Missouri matter —[1959]) holds that although a written contract is not signed by one or both of the parties, the acceptance by one of the performance by the other will give validity to the instrument and impose on the acceptor the corresponding obligation provided therein.

And finally, just to put a cap on this whole flow of legalisms, we can turn to the lawbooks themselves: Williston: *A Treatise on the Law of Contracts*, Third Edition, Section 91, pages 319-322:

> Where the offeree takes or retains possession of property which has been offered to him, such taking or retention in the absence of other circumstances is an acceptance.

Now, let's go to a recent example. A chap in Idaho sends to a New York advertising agency a number of transparencies. No contract is sent to the agency. The request, however, is not un-solicited. The agency specifically requests certain transparencies for possible use by a client of theirs. The transparencies are accompanied by a letter advising that the agency can hold same for a period of two weeks. Nothing is mentioned as to what will happen if the transparencies are lost or damaged.

It turns out that seventeen transparencies are not returned. The agency admits that it received the transparencies but denies that there is any agreement to lease the transparencies or to pay the photographer in the event of loss. The agency simply said that it asked for the transparencies and if its client approved of same, then the photographer would be paid. The photographer moves in court for a summary judgment on the basis that there are no triable issues of fact and that there is no defense to the causes of action. In effect, says the photographer, the liability of the agency is already set. Is the agency liable?

The decision was handed down in the Supreme Court of the State of New York on October 2, 1972 (*Lindholm* v. *Launey*, Index. No. 19981/72). The photographer was granted summary judgment in seeking the recovery or the value of the seventeen transparencies. The Court said:

> The obligation to return was not disputed. That defendant did not know the value of the transparencies is not only unrealistic, but in any case, they were retained, finally misplaced and unreturned.

Although this is a major step, it is not the only step nor the final one. A photographer might quickly think that all he has to do is send transparencies out and not worry about anything else. Remember that the above case details the fact that transparencies were sent at the agency's request and that it admitted the loss of same. The only question then remaining to be decided was not if the agency was liable but rather by how much.

Before moving into how the photographer can protect himself, let's discuss the value of photographs. The same applies to a transparency or a black-and-white negative.

There are certain ways in which this can be determined. One is the actual value of the photograph in question which can be determined by its prior use, the leasing fees commanded and the extent of usage. This means exactly what it says. Suppose you have a transparency that is ten years old. Each year you lease it twice at a fee of $100 each time so that over the ten-year period, that one transparency has brought you $2,000. This sum is compared with the life of a transparency and through some simple computations, it can be readily determined what kind of market value that particular transparency has.

In the absence of market value there is what is known as intrinsic value. This is indeed a rather nebulous term and for many years caused much grief among photographers, mainly because it was difficult to establish. This is becoming less so today. The law in this area is quite specific, even though the area itself is rather general.

The courts have finally established the intrinsic value concept. They have consistently found that while ordinarily the measure of damages for loss of personal property is the value of the property at the time of the loss, absence of market value does not restrict the owner to nominal damages; recourse may be had to some other rational method of ascertaining the value of the property from such elements as are attainable.

Taft v. *Smith, Gray & Co.* (134 NYS 1011 [1912]), a leading case, said that the cost of replacement or reproduction based upon either the actual cash outlay or the value of the necessary labor and materials has been held to constitute the measure of damages of property having no market value. So, therefore, where a transparency has no leasing history, the measure of damages is computed by the intrinsic value of the photograph.

Where does this all come from? Actually, the farthest-reaching and most applicable case is one dating back to the turn of the century. *Wamsley* v. *Atlas Steamship Co.* (50 AD—New York 199) involved the loss of a box of negatives of scenery taken in a foreign land and having no market value. The law in this case is still considered the view today. The Court said:

> That those articles had no market value was quite clearly shown, and when that appeared, the plaintiff was at liberty to give such other evidence as would assist the jury to assess the actual value. That was to be done by showing the nature of the property; the cost of obtaining the photographs; the purpose for which they were procured and the difficulty of replacing them. The jury were also entitled to take into consideration the value of the property to the plaintiff. . . .

But, the court didn't stop there. It had more to say in keeping its decision unclouded.

> The fact that the negatives were not good ones, and were not well taken was, of course, to be considered; but, in addition to that, the jury might also consider that when one has gone a long way to obtain photographs of scenery of a foreign land which is difficult to reach, or where the photograph is of some incident which is not likely to be repeated, even a poor representation may be of considerable value, if a picture can be printed from it, because, as far as it goes, it is a correct representation of what occurred. . . .

As we said before, this is still the law today.

Looking further at market value and intrinsic value, we note the case of *Rhoades, Inc.* v. *United Air Lines, Inc.* (U.S. 224 F. Supp. 341 [1963]), in which it was held that where personal property is without market value, evidence as to cost or other considerations affecting its valuation, real or intrinsic, is admissible to establish value. Again, in another federal case, *King* v. *U.S.* (292 F. Supp. 767 [1968]), it was held that the measure of damages for injury to property without market value is the actual or intrinsic value of the property.

In other words, the value to an owner based on his actual money loss, all circumstances and conditions considered, is standard for finding as to damages for property lacking market value (*Lobell* v. *Paleg*, 154 NYS 2d, 709 [1956]).

We cannot emphasize too strongly that a wrongdoer may not escape liability simply because there is no market value, or none of the ordinary standards for measuring the damages exist. One need only look at *MacGregor* v. *Watts* (254 AD— New York 904 [1938]) in which the complaint charged the loss of manuscript plays, one of which had been copyrighted but which had undergone changes and alterations since the issuance of the copyright.

The court ruled that it would be an error to dismiss the charges on the ground that there was no measure of damages to be applied to the plaintiff's loss; therefore, the plaintiff was entitled to damages. The court said that obviously the plaintiff would be put to some expense in obtaining a copy of the copyrighted book, and further, that she was entitled to recover damages even though she was unable to establish a market value for her property. Again, note that if the property does not have a market value, then, if there is a total loss, the measure of damages is the cost to replace or reproduce the article. If it cannot be reproduced or replaced, its value to the owner may be considered in fixing damages.

One of the most recent of the intrinsic value cases was decided in 1973 in the matter of *Dr. Carlton Ray* v. *The American Museum of Natural History* (Index No. 6980/71—Supreme Court, New York County). Dr. Ray is a well-known scientist and photographer who, in January of 1969, delivered to the American Museum certain rare and unique original color transparencies of indigenous species taken by him in the Antarctica. The American Museum owned and published a magazine entitled *Natural History* and the transpaencies were to be used in that magazine. The Museum failed to return eleven of the transparencies.

Dr. Ray attempted to establish the cost of replacement or reproduction of the transparencies, based upon either the actual cash outlay or the value of the required labor and materials. The transparencies had been taken by Dr. Ray while on an expedition in the Antarctica. Therefore, under the above-cited cases, the measure of damages for injury to property without a market value would be the actual or intrinsic value of the property.

Furthermore, it had been found under case law that just because the value was speculative, uncertain, even difficult to prove, there was no ground for denying any recovery or for limiting such recovery to nominal damages only.

Dr. Ray in his testimony told the court about (1) the remoteness of the location where the transparencies were taken, (2) the fact that the transparencies were taken underwater which involved extreme hazards, (3) they were the best of what he took and (4) they had data value. Data value means it is absolutely impossible to reproduce the conditions when the picture was first taken.

The decision was handed down in the Supreme Court of the State of New York. The court determined that the fair and reasonable value of the transparencies was $15,000. There was no appeal taken and the plaintiff received that sum. Once more, note that if the property does not have a market value, and, if there is a total loss, the measure of damages is the cost to replace or reproduce the article. If it cannot be reproduced or replaced, then its value to the owner may be considered in fixing damages. This is what the Ray case showed.

We have now seen the functions of market and intrinsic values. The next determination of the value of a photograph can be via the use of a stipulated damage provision.

A stipulated damage provision is exactly what it says it is: a provision stipulating damages. Stipulated damages means the compensation which the parties agreed in advance would be paid for loss or injury that follows a breach of contract. The purpose of a stipulated damage provision is quite apparent: it is to permit the parties to look to the future, anticipate that there may be a breach and arrange for a settlement in advance. The parties to a contract do have the right to include any stipulation which they may agree upon, provided it is not unconscionable or contrary to public policy; in other words, no rule of law forbids them from agreeing between themselves as to the amount of damages anticipated.

To recap, where there is a clause in a contract calling for payment of a stipulated sum in the event of breach of contract, its effect is to substitute the amount agreed upon for the actual damages resulting from the breach of the contract and thereby prevent controversy between the parties as to the amount of damages.

As of this writing, the loss of or damage to a single original transparency can be stipulated at $1500. A number of elements back up this figure. For example, custom and usage in the trade.

Rose Inn Corp. v. *National Union Ins.* (258 NY 51 [1932]) holds that evidence of usage in a particular trade has been admissible with other circumstances to prove assent or justifiable inference from silence. Additionally, where parties have had mutual dealings and one renders to the other a statement purporting to set forth all the items of indebtedness on one side and credit on the other, the account so rendered, if not objected to in a reasonable time, becomes an account stated and cannot afterwards be impeached except for fraud or mistake. See how this dovetails with the law reached on liability previously detailed in this section.

New York has established the value of photographs today and the $1500 figure for transparencies is within that range. In fact, the $1500 figure for a lost or damaged transparency has

been adjudicated seven different times in seven different arbitration decisions before seven different arbitrators.

The courts in New York have continued to hold for the
stipulated damage provision. In one Civil Court matter (*Alpha
& FPG* v. *Pacific Lithograph Co.*, Index No. 76687/72, decided
on October 30, 1974), the court found that the fair and reasonable value of each of fifteen transparencies of dogs and cats is
$500. This is exactly what plaintiffs sued for. Not only did the
court award the full amount of the suit, but it also granted interest from the date the defendant failed to return the transparencies.

Again, as with the Ray case, no appeal was taken and the
judgment was paid. But, the changes in the law for this area of
photography doesn't just stop with decisions on transparencies.
Even black-and-white positive prints . . . that's right . . .
black-and-white positive prints have jumped into the act.

In the matter of *Photo Researchers* v. *Careccia* (Index No.
58451/74), the Civil Court in the City of New York set $100 for
the loss of a black-and-white positive print. Case law has also
held that the measure of damages is based on custom and
usage in the industry as to what charges are normally placed
for a detention of a photograph.

This is an area known as holding fees. Let's take an example.
The case was *Photo Researchers* v. *Norman, Craig & Kummel*
(Civil Court, New York, Index No. 57634/69), wherein the defendant, a well-known advertising agency, held transparencies
beyond a two-week period. The court held that there were no
triable issues except as to the amount due the plaintiff and
that this could be determined on an assessment.

Remember, then, a person dealing in a particular market will
be taken to have dealt according to the generally recognized
customs or rules of the market, whether he is in fact aware of
the practices or not.

The decision handed down on August 21, 1969, said that the
defendant ". . . admits that these transparencies were delivered to it on March 29, 1968 and the same were not returned to
plaintiff until March 4, 1969. It matters not whether defendant
is an insurer or a bailee."

Now, what happens when the laboratory is the culprit?
Where it loses or damages the material?

Let's look at two cases which control today.

Goor v. *Navillo* (31 NYS 2d 619) was decided in 1941. Plaintiff took pictures on his vacation and gave them to the defendant for processing. The carton which contained the film had the following inscription: "The film in this carton has been made with great care and will be processed in our laboratory without additional charge. If we find this film to have been defective in manufacture or to have been damaged in our laboratory we will replace it, but we assume no other responsibility either expressed or implied."

It was held that the recovery was limited to damages equal to the replacement costs of the film, because the carton containing the film bore the clear and conspicuous inscription stated above.

The court also found that there was an absence of evidence to show that the plaintiff was either illiterate, blind or ignorant of the language on the carton, or that the inscription was misread or misrepresented to him. Pay attention to the fact that the only way to get around this limited liability would be to show that it was a penalty and not stipulated damages.

Willard Van Dyke Productions v. *Eastman Kodak* (228 NYS 2d 330) was decided in 1963. The facts are similar to the Goor case except that on the carton of film there was a legend that the price of the film did not include processing. Accordingly, the court found that the limitation was not binding on the photographer whose film was ruined in the processing.

What the court was saying here is that the limitation at the time of the purchase of the film applied solely to that purchase and did not carry over into the separate transaction for processing. Therefore, said the court, in the absence of clear proof that the liability limitation was agreed upon as part of the processing contract, the photographer was not to be barred from recovering the full amount of the damages he suffered as a result of the ruining of his film. It is interesting to note that the court implies there would be a limitation of liability if it were made part of the processing contract.

This case in particular had two offshoots concerning accord and satisfaction which are interesting to note.

An exception (with limitations) was taken in 1964 in the case of *Velsicol Chemical Corp.* v. *Hooker Chemical Corp.* (230 F. Supp. 998). The court held that where the amount due was in dispute and payment was submitted in full satisfaction of the obligation and accepted with that understanding, an accord and satisfaction resulted.

In 1969, however, the matter of *Bassett* v. *Bassett* (31 AD 2d 779) added another twist and cited Van Dyke specifically. A partnership was dissolved and the plaintiff received two checks for $20,000 and $21,093.98 respectively, representing repayment of his contribution of capital to the partnership and payment of his share of earnings and profits. Set forth on each check was a legend stating in substance that endorsement of the instrument would constitute a release of all claims arising out of plaintiff's interest in the partnership. Plaintiff refused to endorse the checks and brought an action, the essential part of the complaint being that defendant, by placing the restrictive legend on the checks, had in effect converted the amounts of the checks. The pleadings failed to establish that plaintiff had been damaged. The amounts represented by the checks were concededly due plaintiff and under the law, payment of an admitted liability is not payment of or consideration for an alleged accord and satisfaction of another and independent liability.

It is the last phrase that falls within the Van Dyke case. Now, let's look at another case, one which is now being discussed for litigation.

A photographer shoots a number of rolls of film out West. He delivers the film to a camera shop and receipts are given. The laboratory damages the film. However, they say it was a force majeure (or act of God) situation and in any event, the receipts for the film limit the liability of the lab to replacement film. Looking at the two main cases quoted above, where does this matter now fall? Clearly, the present matter falls within the Van Dyke case in that there is a limitation of liability in the processing receipts. However, two factors should be considered: (1) Is the limited liability language a penalty rather than stipulated damages, especially in view of the intrinsic value of the transparencies? (2) Is there really clear proof that the limitation of liability was agreed upon as part of the processing arrangement?

Also to be considered is whether the lab's language in its receipts might just be against public policy, especially in light of the kind of pictures that were submitted and by whom? And perhaps the most tantalizing question of all, if liability is indeed found, what is the value then of unprocessed film? The case is now in litigation and we are just as anxious as you to know the results.

Now we come to the area of protection. How does a photographer fully and completely protect himself? One is to use a delivery memo whenever a submission is made. What kind of delivery memo? Well, there are many floating around. The most common one we have seen is the following:

DELIVERY MEMO

Photographer's Name: Date:

Address: Telephone No.:

To:

Enclosed please find: No. of Units: Kindly check count and acknowledge by signing and mailing this copy. Count shall be considered correct if copy is not received by return mail.

TERMS OF DELIVERY

1. Photographs are submitted for 14 days approval. Unless a longer period is requested, and granted by me in writing, a holding fee of $5 per week per color transparency and $1 per week per black-and-white positive will be charged against such 14-day period and up to the time of return.

2. Photographs may not be used in any way, until submission of invoice indicating sale of right to use the same, which shall be only on terms of use hereinafter specified.

3. Projection of transparencies is not permitted. This delivery is not considered a bailment and is specifically conditioned upon the item so delivered being returned to me in the same condition as delivered. You assume an insurer's liability herein for the safe and undamaged return of the photographs to me. Such photographs are to be returned by bonded messenger, or registered mail, return receipt requested, fully insured.

4. The monetary damage for loss or damage of an original color transparency or photograph shall be determined by the value of each individual photograph. You agree, however, that the agreed and reasonable minimum value of such lost or damaged photograph or transparency shall be no less than $1,500.

5. Any objection to terms are to be made in writing within

ten (10) days from receipt of this delivery memo. Such terms and conditions are made pursuant to Article 2 of the Uniform Commercial Code.

6. Any and all disputes arising out, under or in connection with this memo, including without limitation, the validity, interpretation, performance and breach hereof, shall be settled by arbitration in pursuant to the rules of the American Arbitration Association. . . . Judgment upon the award rendered may be entered in the highest court of the Forum, State or Federal, having jurisdiction. This delivery memo, its validity and effect shall be interpreted under and governed by the laws of the State of. . . . You shall pay all costs of arbitration, plus legal interests of any award.

(Photographer)

Once a photograph is sold, then it comes time to bill the user. This involves the use of an invoice. Again, the one we have seen most commonly in use is the following:

INVOICE

("User")   Invoice #
                    (Re Delivery Memo #   )

Attention: Date

RIGHTS GRANTED: One-time, nonexclusive reproduction rights to the photographs listed herein.

TYPE OF USE:
(As Defined on Reverse Side)

DISTRIBUTION TERRITORY:

LANGUAGE:

SIZE OF PHOTOS IN USE: Photographs shall not be used in a size greater than the size set forth below, wherever and whenever used.

SPECIAL ARRANGEMENTS:

DESCRIPTION OF PHOTOGRAPHS

Size of Use	Photo Code #	Color (C)	Black & White (B&W)	Fee
				TOTAL FEE:

The Definition of Rights and the Terms and Conditions set forth on the reverse side are deemed incorporated herein and made a part hereof.

ANY OBJECTION TO TERMS ARE TO BE MADE IN WRITING WITHIN TEN (10) DAYS FROM RECEIPT OF THIS INVOICE. SUCH TERMS AND CONDITIONS ARE MADE PURSUANT TO ARTICLE 2 OF THE UNIFORM COMMERCIAL CODE.

TERMS AND CONDITIONS OF USE

1. A) Photographs and transparencies (hereafter "photographs") remain the property of   . User does not acquire any right, title or interest in or to any photograph, including, without limitation, any electronic or promotional right, and will not make, authorize or permit any use of the particular photograph(s) or plate(s) made therefrom, other than as specified herein. All photographs are to be returned within four (4) months after date of this invoice, except in cases of outright purchase.

B) User agrees to pay as reasonable charges the sum of Five Dollars ($5.00) per week per color transparency and One Dollar ($1.00) per week per black-and-white positive, to   after such four (4) month period, to date of return.

2. User is solely responsible for loss or damage to photographs and will indemnify against any such loss or damage, commencing with receipt by user of such photograph until its return to, and receipt by,   . In this connection, User assumes an insurer's liability herein for the safe and undamaged return of the photographs to   . Such photographs are only to be returned either by bonded messenger or by registered mail (return receipt requested), prepaid and fully insured.

3. The monetary damage for loss or damage of a photograph shall be determined by the value of such photograph. User agrees that the reasonable minimum value of such lost or damaged photograph shall be no less than Fifteen Hundred Dollars ($1,500) for a color transparency or black-and-white negative. User acknowledges that this clause is essential and material to the making of this agreement. User shall be liable for all acts of its employees, agents, assigns, messengers and free-lance researchers for all loss, damage or misuse of the photographs.

4. Photographs used editorially shall bear a credit line as indictated by   . User shall provide copyright protection to the photograph granted to it. Such copyright shall be immediately assigned to   , upon his request without charge.

5. No model releases or other releases exist on any pho-

107

tographs unless the existence of such release is specified in writing by   . User shall indemnify   against all claims arising out of the use of any photographs where the existence of such release has not been specified in writing by   . In any event, the limit of liability of   shall be the sum paid to him pursuant to this invoice for the use of the particular photograph involved.

6. This agreement is not assignable or transferable on the part of the User.

7. Time is of the essence in the performance by User of its obligations for payments and return of photographs hereunder. No rights are granted until payment is made to   even though User has received this invoice.

8. Only the terms of use herein set forth shall be binding upon   . No purported waiver of any of the terms herein shall be binding on   unless subscribed to in writing by

9. Payment herein for such use is to be net ten (10) days. A service charge of one-and-one-half (1½%) percent per month on any unpaid balance will be charged thereafter. Any claims for adjustment or rejection of terms must be made to   within ten (10) days after receipt of this invoice. In the event that any photographs are used by User in publications, then User shall send to   , on a semiannual basis (June 30 and December 31), a certified statement setting forth the total number of sales, sublicenses, adaptations, translations and any other uses. User shall provide   with two (2) free copies of such publication immediately upon printing.

10. All rights not specifically granted herein to User are reserved for   's use and disposition without any limitations whatsoever.

DISPUTES OR CLAIMS ARISING OUT OF USE

11. Any and all disputes arising out of, under or in connection with this agreement, including without limitation, the validity, interpretation, performance and breach hereof, shall be settled by arbitration in   , pursuant to the rules of the American Arbitration Association. Judgment upon the award rendered may be entered in the highest court of the Forum, State or Federal, having jurisdiction. This agreement, its validity and effect shall be interpreted under and governed by the laws of the State of   . The User shall pay all costs of arbitration, plus legal interest on any award.

12. No electronic reproduction rights or promotional rights are granted herein, unless specifically stated.

13. User agrees that the above terms are made pursuant to Article 2 of the Uniform Commercial Code and agrees to be bound by same.

TO SUMMARIZE

Liability is determined by the contractual arrangements between the parties. Absence of a contract relegates the photographer to the other areas of the law for collection purposes.

Damages are proved in three ways: the market value, the intrinsic value and the stipulated value.

9

Do I Need an Agent?

Some photographers need agents. Some photographers need special kinds of agents. And, of course, some photographers are their own best agents.

An agent is a representative, someone who represents the photographer with respect to the disposition of his work. According to Webster, an agent is defined as "one who or that which acts; one that exerts power or has the power to act; a person entrusted with the business of another." Note that last phrase. "A person entrusted with the business of another." In the photography field, there are primarily two kinds of agents: the individual one and the stock house. The former is exactly that: an individual who handles the work of the photographer. A party who takes the photographer's work and through his contacts tries to sell, license or otherwise dispose of such materials. Years ago, there used to be many personal agents in the photography field. The number has dwindled considerably. The reason for this is that the photographer has become more experienced and adept in dealing with the disposition of his photographs; accordingly, the necessity of having a personal representative has decreased. Secondly, the stock agency has risen dramatically and these agencies are dealing with matters that once were the sole bailiwick of the individual photo agent.

What then is a stock agency? How does it function? A stock agency is an organization which handles photographs in bulk. That is, it is an agency for the sale of a product rather than simply a service.

Let's take an example. Suppose you, the photographer, have shot some five hundred pictures of unicycles in Thailand. You have been trying to interest someone in buying them. Nobody bites. So, you take your four hundred color transparencies and one hundred black-and-white negatives to a stock agency (they are also known as stock libraries, stock houses, picture agencies, etc.). The agency looks over your work, decides if it is of merit to them (meaning, can they sell it?) and decides to handle your work. Now, understand one thing. A stock agency doesn't have to be a huge outfit on the top floor of 666 Fifth Avenue. The agency can be anything from three people working out of a hall closet to fifty people in a penthouse suite. Their function is still the same: to select the best of what you have to offer and then make that product available to potential users. Users are book publishers, advertisers, magazines, newspapers, etc.

If the agency decides to handle your work, you will be given what is termed an "Exclusive Agency Contract" to sign. In effect, such a contract gives the agency the exclusive right to represent you with respect to the materials involved, for a specific period of time, in return for which the agency will receive a certain commission based on what they do with the materials. That's the crux of the contract. Naturally, it is much longer than that when "reduced" to writing. The average contract will specifically set forth the fact that the photographer is appointing the agency as his sole and exclusive agent with respect to the sale and leasing of the particular materials. The reason for the "sole and exclusive" language is self-explanatory. The agency doesn't want to wind up in competition with someone else, including you. If they are going to represent you, then they want to make sure that they are not going to expend a lot of time and effort in your behalf only to have you undercut them by selling the same materials elsewhere.

What the agency receives in the way of a commission varies. The usual fee has been 50%. This means that the agency receives 50% of the total sums billed and collected by them with respect to the disposition of your work.

There are a number of provisions in the standard agency contract, some of which can be considered "standard" in the industry and some of which are open to negotiation. As with all agreements, everything is really open to negotiation; but inasmuch as the photographer is turning over to the agency his original work, he should read the agreement carefully and be sure he understands it. After all, the agency will now be holding such original materials; therefore, this situation is quite a bit different with respect to the area of liability in case of loss or damage than the principles set forth in the preceding chapter.

The agency and you reach agreement. You turn over the selected materials. The agency now catalogs those materials in its existing files. Some agencies have more elaborate files than others. One agency may use a simple index card procedure in filing your work, while another may utilize the services of a computer and special filing cabinets. In any event, your work is generally amalgamated into the agency's existing files. This means that, for the most part, if you have delivered all 500 shots of unicycles in Thailand, plus maybe 123 shots of porcupines and 79 shots of Rome's Coliseum, those pictures will be incorporated in the agency's present files on unicycles in Thailand, porcupines and the Coliseum.

What happens thereafter is relatively simple.

An advertising agency may call the stock house. "Hey, Charley, you got any pictures of unicycles in Thailand?"

Pay dirt!

The agency turns to its files and culls the shots of unicycles in Thailand. It just so happens that the agency specializes in that field and it pulls out 5,473 pictures of unicycles, of which 500 are yours.

The advertising agency usually has a period of two weeks in which to decide which, if any, of the shots it wishes to utilize. After that period, the holding fee mentioned in Chapter 8 becomes applicable.

Now, on the thirteenth day, the advertising agency selects one of the transparencies which it desires to utilize in an ad for travel to Thailand. A price is negotiated between the stock agency and the advertising agency for the reproduction of the transparency. The advertising agency will arrange to reproduce that transparency for use in the particular brochure and the original transparency will then be returned to the stock agency and be put back in the files.

The advertising agency is billed with an invoice similar to the one described in Chapter 8. The face of the invoice would probably contain the following:

To: Aardvark Advertising Agency
    111 Binding Way
    Anytown, U.S.A.

For the one-time, nonexclusive reproduction rights to the following photograph for use in a brochure entitled "Let's Ride to Thailand," up to a printing of 5,999 copies:

1 color, 35mm transparency, #1A234, of 14 people on a unicycle, by Peter Photographer.

Price: $_____

When the price is paid to the stock agency, that organization will then deduct its commission, pursuant to the terms of its contract with you and remit the balance to you.

That is basically how the procedure operates.

Some stock agencies also get involved with other uses of the photographer's work such as filmstrips, etc. They also handle claims when materials are not returned on time or are returned in a damaged state, as well as protecting the interests of the photographer in general.

The question most often asked is whether stock houses really handle anything more than the photographer's "excess" work or nondescript stock pictures. The answer is, not necessarily. Some agencies, like some personal representatives, specialize in a particular brand of product. Some agencies are more artistic than others; some, of course, handle things in bulk. You have to pretty much seek out and decide what agency may be best for you. There are plenty to choose from. For example, LMP (*Literary Market Place*), published by R. R. Bowker Co., lists in its 1975-76 edition 97 photo and picture sources, half of these being in New York City alone.

There are agencies, it should be noted, who don't just deal in what the photographer has left with them. They also deal in assignment work.

Suppose, for example, Adam Agent sitting at his lightbox receives a call from his good friend Arnold Argonaut at the Aardvark Advertising Agency one bright Sunday morning. "Adam, I have a problem. I need a good shot of a unicycle in Thailand, similar to what you gave me before, but this time I only want eleven people on the bike."

"No problem, Arnold, I'll have Peter Photographer take care of it. He's the best there is on shooting cluttered unicycles."

So, they agree on an arrangement for the cost of such an assignment and Adam Agent then contacts the photographer. Now, the original standard contract which the agency and the photographer entered into may not cover this area of assignments. Therefore, the agency submits a separate agreement. The typical agreement between itself and the photographer may look like this:

Date: _____

To: Adam Agency
New York, New York

Gentlemen: Re: Assignment for Unicycles in Thailand

The following represents the agreement between you and me:

I hereby acknowledge that I am an independent contractor with respect to my relationship with you on the above photographic assignment. Any and all acts or omissions done by me are my sole responsibility. I will use my best efforts to complete the assignment and all sums due as a result of this assignment will be the sole responsibility of the person or organization for whom I am doing the work and not you.

I also acknowledge that you and your agency were instrumental in obtaining said assignment and, therefore, for your services rendered, you shall:

1. Be entitled to your agency commission which shall be _____; and
2. Have exclusive agency rights with respect to the transparencies or photographs taken on such assignment and not utilized by the principal party for whom I am doing the assignment, for a period of five (5) years from the date of submission of such materials to you.

I shall hold you and your agency and their assigns, licensees and legal representatives, harmless from any and all claims arising out of the assignment or omissions caused by me with respect to the assignment and the photographs or transparencies taken on such assignment.

Very truly yours,

_____

Confirmed: Peter Photographer
Adam Agency

By: _____

Again, although we said it was typical, this agreement is open to negotiation and may include other provisions which the photographer (or the agency) may want. Naturally, some provisions may be deleted, depending on the deal made.

Let's look at another side. Suppose, the advertising agency already knows of Peter Photographer. Maybe the photographer worked for the agency some years ago. In this instance, our friend Arnold Argonaut may call the photographer directly: "Peter, old buddy, I have an assignment for you."

It is now up to Peter to protect himself. The Delivery Memo and Invoice which we detailed in the preceding section are really not on target with these new facts. So, there is another form which the photographer should have at his disposal; this is known as an Assignment Agreement. As stated previously, each photographer has his own form and his own way of doing things. The form set forth here is simply the type of form we have seen in use by a number of photographers. If there is something you need inserted, then insert it. If there is something you need deleted, then delete it.

Attachment—Exhibit "B"

EXHIBIT "B"

TERMS OF ASSIGNMENT

To: _____

Date:_____

Dear _____

You hereby engage the undersigned _____
to render photographic services for you as follows:

Date of Services:
Length of Services:
Nature of Services:
Fee to Be Paid:
Expenses to Be Paid:
   Travel
   Per Diem
   Assistance
   Film & Processing
   Other

Number and Size of Photographs Required:
Color or Black and White:
Special Arrangements:
Rights to Be Granted:
 One or More Times
 Exclusive/Nonexclusive
 Territory
 Manner of Reproduction

Terms and Conditions

1. All transparencies and photographs (herein collectively called "photographs") remain my property and, except as specifically set forth above, you do not acquire any other right, title or interest in or to any photograph.

2. You are solely responsible for loss or damage to photographs and will indemnify me against any loss or damage, commencing with receipt by you of such photographs until their return to, and receipt by, me. In this connection, you assume an insurer's liability herein for the safe and undamaged return of the photographs to me. Such photographs are only to be returned either by messenger or by registered mail (return receipt requested), prepaid and fully insured.

3. The monetary damage for loss or damage of a photograph shall be determined by the value of such photograph. If the photograph so lost or damaged has no market value in that there has been no prior use, then in the absence of market value, the monetary damage shall be determined by the intrinsic value of such photograph. You shall be liable for all acts of your employees, agents, assigns, messengers and freelance researchers for all loss, damage or misuse of the photographs.

4. Photographs used editorially shall bear a credit line to me. If there is a failure to provide such a credit line, then I shall be entitled to twice the fee set forth above. You shall provide copyright protection to the photograph granted to you. Such copyright shall be immediately assigned to me, upon my request, without charge.

5. If requested, I shall provide model releases on any photographs delivered to you provided such photographs warrant such releases. You shall indemnify me against all claims arising out of the use of any photographs where the existence of such release has not been requested in writing by you. In any event, the limit of my liability shall be the sum paid to me pursuant to this agreement for the use of the particular photograph involved.

116

6. This agreement is not assignable or transferrable on your part.

7. Time is of the essence in the performance by you of your obligations for payments and return of photographs hereunder. All payments must be made within thirty (30) days from the date hereof.

8. Only the terms herein set forth shall be binding upon me. No purported waiver of any of the terms herein shall be binding on me unless subscribed in writing by me.

9. All rights not specifically granted herein to you are reserved for my use and disposition without any limitation whatsoever.

10. Any and all disputes arising out of, under or in connection with this agreement, including without limitation the validity, interpretation, performance and breach hereof, shall be settled by arbitration in _____, pursuant to the rules of the American Arbitration Association. Judgment upon the award rendered may be entered in the highest court of the Forum, State or Federal, having jurisdiction. This agreement, its validity and effect shall be interpreted under and governed by the laws of the State of _____. You shall pay all costs of arbitration, plus legal interest on any award.

11. You agree that the above terms are made pursuant to Article 2 of the UNIFORM COMMERCIAL CODE and you agree to be bound by same.

Please signify your acceptance and agreement to the terms herein contained by signing and returning same herewith.

Very truly yours,

_____

Agreed to and Accepted:

_____

Finally, while we are on this whole subject of agencies and assignments, let's touch briefly on the functions of certain guilds. There are a number of them around the country, some with specialized interests. There are the Professional Photographers Association of America, the American Society of Picture Professionals, IPANY (the Industrial Photographers Association of New York, LIPPA (the Long Island Professional Photographers Association and the Society of Photographic Education, to mention but a few. One need only look in the local phone book for their numbers or ask around to obtain information on what these various organizations do. Most of them are extremely valuable in disseminating information about the photography field. Many hold frequent meetings to discuss various aspects of the field. They print and distribute publications. There are symposiums, conferences, etc. A few of the more prominent conferences are the Wilson Hicks Conference in Miami, the Southern Short Course in News Photography in Boone, North Carolina, the Visual Communications Conference at the University of Maryland and the Minnesota Symposium on Visual Communication at the University of Minnesota. Each offers a wide range of information with lectures by and discussions with some of the most prominent people in the photographic field.

The American Society of Magazine Photographers (ASMP)—now known as the Society of Photographers in Communications, located in New York City, with chapters throughout the country, is an organization comprised of about twelve hundred of the world's leading professional photographers in journalism, advertising, fashion, books, television, film and other media. Its primary objective is to promote the interests of photographers and although we are not specifically saying that this organization is the only one to turn to, it is common knowledge that they have been a leading voice in photographers' rights. The organization also publishes a *Business Practices Guide*, which details certain contract forms, procedures and photo pricing.

TO SUMMARIZE

Whether a photographer requires an agent depends pretty much on the individual circumstances of the photographer. If he does, then he must know the basis of the representation by the agent. As with anything else, it is imperative that the photographer understand clearly the many agreements and relationships which he may have with agents and other users of photography, whether it be advertising agencies, magazine and newspaper publishers or even Mr. & Mrs. Smith who want photographs taken of their 40th anniversary. There is also a wealth of information available to the photographer and he need only ask for it through the various guilds and associations.

10

How Do I Function If I'm a Studio Photographer?

Let's turn to that one class of photographer whom almost everyone has dealt with at one time or another. It is the studio photographer. He is the one who works in a studio—obviously—or operates from it. This can apply to any photographer, but a studio photographer is generally classified as one who takes portraits, bar mitzvahs, weddings, confirmations, etc.

Photography is unrestricted, so that there are advertising (commercial) photographers who are also portrait photographers and news photographers (photo journalists) who can photograph a wedding with the best of them. But for the most part, a studio photographer is one who may have a studio on Main Street and who is engaged by local people to photograph various social functions such as the ones enumerated above.

The prime thing the studio photographer must remember is that he is really an employee—most of the time. He is retained to take photographs. That being the case, he must be especially cognizant of who owns what. For you studio photographers, reread Chapter 2. Remember, absence of an agreement to the contrary, the employer, the sitter, the customer owns everything. The studio photographer then must make sure he has that "agreement to the contrary."

Again, each photographer has his own special way of doing things. There is usually little problem with the face of most of the forms the photographer uses in this field. They contain the customary information as to the job description: the number of prints to be made, the type of work to be done (e.g., albums, separates), the price to be paid, the deposit involved, place of engagement, etc. It is when the photographer gets to the reverse side—the terms and conditions—that complications can result.

The language here is relatively easy to understand and this is an example of the kind of language we have seen. Naturally, the photographer will have to tailor-make its provisions to his needs:

TERMS & PROVISIONS

1. All photographic materials (negatives, proofs, transparencies, etc.) shall remain the sole and exclusive property of Peter's Studio. The ordering party shall be permitted the right to order prints of such materials (subject to approval of Peter's Studio) at the agreed-to prevailing rate.

2. If the ordering party fails to make whatever payments are required under this agreement, then all obligations, if any, of Peter's Studio shall cease without any further obligation thereto to the ordering party.

3. With respect to all payments hereunder, a service charge of _____ percent per month on any unpaid balance shall be charged. If collection is necessary, the ordering party shall be solely responsible for all collection costs, including reasonable counsel fees. Time is deemed of the essence with respect to all payments hereunder.

4. No trade custom or trade usage shall be deemed to affect the terms of this agreement.

5. There shall be no liability on behalf of Peter's Studio, its employees, agents, assigns or licensees, for their nonperformance caused by any force majeure or similar circumstances, illness, accident or any other cause beyond their control; nor for the loss or damage or destruction of any photographic materials (whether they be negatives, proofs, prints, transparencies, etc.) and whether in transit or in developing. In any event, the limit of Peter's Studio's liability shall not exceed the contract price stated herein.

6. Peter's Studio shall deliver proofs or prints to the ordering party in accordance with those standards reasonably deemed acceptable throughout the industry. Failure of the ordering party to object, in writing, to such proofs or prints within ten (10) days after receipt, shall constitute a waiver.

7. No warranty is made as to the color clarity or fidelity of color prints. Acceptance of prints or albums of whatsoever kind shall be deemed a release of all claims against Peter's Studio, its employees, agents, assigns, licensees or legal representatives.

8. This agreement is not to be construed as an employment agreement in any way. Peter's Studio's function is that of an independent contractor.

9. No changes in any part of this agreement (except for the completion of blank spaces) shall be deemed valid or binding. There are no oral or other agreements or representations by and between the parties hereto and this agreement shall constitute the full and complete agreement between the parties.

10. This agreement shall be governed solely by the laws of the State of _____. Any litigation arising therefrom shall be conducted in the State of _____.

11. Peter's Studio shall have the right to display or publish any of the photographs taken pursuant to this agreement and the ordering party hereby consents and agrees to same.

12. There shall be no refunds of any monies paid if the engagement hereunder is cancelled in any way. The full and complete sum shall be deemed due and owing at the completion of the engagement hereunder, notwithstanding the subsequent selection of prints.

The studio photographer has his own specialized problems. Since he is in business as an entrepreneur in addition to being a creator of artistic work, he must be fully aware of the many areas of the law that apply to him.

For example, with the concurrence of his accountant, it is, in many cases, advisable for the studio photographer to incorporate his business to avoid risking his personal possessions. After he has done this, he must be concerned with the lease for his studio. It would be an understatement to say that the lease must permit the type of business the photographer is entering into. Additionally, a qualified broker should be consulted about insurance problems. There is always the possibility of a customer tripping on the premises or otherwise finding himself entangled with a camera or a light fixture.

What happens when the photographer covers social functions? We've even seen a photographer trip over the guest of honor at a bar mitzvah. Also, there are many instances where an individual photographer will hire, as an employee, another photographer to shoot an affair for him or in conjunction with him because of the size and magnitude of the engagement. The studio photographer must protect himself against possible damaging acts of the individual contractor.

A very serious problem arises, for example, when a photographer shoots an entire take of a wedding and sends it off to be processed, only to find that the film is ruined by the laboratory. What steps have been taken by the photographer to protect himself from liability to the wedding party? In addition, what steps can the photographer take against the laboratory? We refer you to Chapter 8 relating to loss and damage of film.

The one suggestion we could make at this time (in view of the existing law) is that the studio photographer purchase film without the cost of processing included, and that when he brings the film to be processed, he make sure that the receipt does not limit the liability of the laboratory.

As indicated above, the problems of studio photographers exceed the bounds of the so-called "normal photography law." They also extend into other areas of law such as lease law, real estate law, corporate law, agency law—all of which can be answered only by a specialist.

Studio photographers should also be aware of the fact that they may utilize the photograph of any of their subjects in a window of their store for display purposes. However, if a customer objects to the use of such a photograph, the photographer must immediately remove such photograph from the display. This is the law of the State of New York and we are sure that similar laws exist in other jurisdictions throughout the country.

TO SUMMARIZE

The studio photographer should be well aware of the fact that the general proposition of law relegates the ownership of all the photographs in a take to the customer. In order to overcome the harshness of the law, it is necessary for the studio photographer to consider using an agreement such as the form set forth in this chapter, or an acceptable variation of the same. Failure to do so can bring hardship and misery to the photographer.

11

Am I Liable
for Misrepresentation?

Two sets of facts:

One: You, the photographer, are asked to take a picture of two salesmen who allegedly earned $2000 each a month in their spare time by selling encyclopedias. You do this. The pictures are used in a magazine extolling the virtues of selling for the encyclopedia company. The problem is that the book company winds up in court for misleading the public. What everybody (meaning the public) took to be two "average" people who earned a goodly sum of money in their "spare" time were really the company's two top salesmen, working *full* time.

The question here is: are you, the photographer, liable for misrepresentation?

Two: You, the photographer, are asked to take a picture of a house which the builder is trying to sell. However, to make that $10,000 shack more appealing, the builder requests that you do a little fancy shooting—like taking one shot from an airplane with gobs and gobs of greenery surrounding the house, or another from a particular angle to show the best aspects of the house. By the time you finish shooting from a number of angles, superimposing shots and using your airbrush with great frequency, the house looks like a $65,000 job.

Question: Any liability on your part here?

Now, before we talk about the answers to these specific problems, let's talk about the field of misrepresentation in general. We are in an area known as truth-in-advertising. It is an area on which the consumer's attention has been focused rather recently. And it is not a simple one.

Books upon books have been written on truth-in-advertising. Almost every day another article reaches the public via newspapers and magazines.

What we will try to do is to give you a basic sketch of what this area is and how the photographer stands in it.

First of all, understand one thing. There is a governmental body which regulates advertising and promotional practices. This is the Federal Trade Commission. It was originally created by an act of Congress in 1914. This act was passed in order to supplement the sanctions concerning unfair competition which had previously been provided by the Sherman Anti-Trust Act of 1890 and the Clayton Act, also of 1914.

What is the Federal Trade Commission? The FTC is composed of five commissioners appointed by the president with the advice and consent of the Senate. No more than three of the commissioners may be selected from the same political party.

So that there is no mistake in its concept, the FTC is not a private party; it is a body charged with the public interest. The act of 1914 specifically directed the FTC to prevent persons from using "unfair methods of competition in commerce and unfair or deceptive acts or practices in commerce" (15 U.S.C.A. 45). This act also explicitly makes "persons," "partnerships" and "corporations" liable for deceptive advertising.

There is no hard and fast rule for determining what an "unfair or deceptive act or practice" is or what a "false advertisement" is. Congress intentionally left the application and interpretation of those terms to the FTC, subject to review by the courts, to enable the FTC to cope with new advertising and merchandising practices as they arose or were brought to light.

"False advertising" is a phrase heard frequently today. It means an advertisement which is misleading in a material respect. To determine if an advertisement is misleading, one has to consider not only representations made or suggested by words, photographs, sounds, etc., but also the extent to which the advertisement fails to reveal facts material to such representations. The Commission and the courts have long held that an advertisement is deceptive if it has the "tendency" or "capacity" to deceive the public (*Charles of the Ritz* v. *FTC*, 143 F2d

676—2d Cir—1944). Proof of actual deception, however, is not required in a Commission case. Using its expertise, the Commission may examine an advertisement and determine its potential effect on the minds of consumers without resorting to a sampling of public opinion or even hearing evidence by the complaining party (*Montgomery Ward* v. *FTC*, 379 F2d 666—7th Cir.—1967). And finally, the Commission may even find an advertisement is violating the FTC Act notwithstanding testimony by consumers that they personally would not be misled (*Double Eagle Lubricants* v. *FTC*, 360 F2d 268—10th Cir.—1965).

In other words, each FTC advertising case revolves around this central issue: is the advertisement unfair or deceptive within the meaning of the FTC Act?

Now, let's back up a little and see what has happened with respect to this field over the years since 1914.

Often when we talk about deceptive advertising, we are talking about fraud. Because of the nature of fraud, and the incredibly different factual possibilities involving it, a number of parties, under certain sets of facts, will be held for its consequences. And this includes the photographer, as we shall soon see. Understand, too, that the fact that a party is acting as an agent or representative does not automatically exonerate him from liability.

At common law, there is a practice known as "puffing." This means that the seller could use extravagant language to obtain the sale. Most of the time, he would not be liable if the seller and buyer were dealing at arm's length and the buyer had equal means of information so as to be qualified to judge the value of the property being sold. Of course, as business grew, so did "puffing." But there reaches a point past which the dramatic becomes the deceptive. Such procedures became so extensive in the advertising industry that local governments had to step in to regulate the practice to protect the public.

That's exactly what is happening today. The various regulatory bodies of government (whether local, state or federal) are taking more action on behalf of the consumer.

In 1922, a case came before the Commission, which has since been designated as the "breakthrough case." For a goodly number of years, the Winsted Hosiery Company had been selling underwear in cartons labeled "Natural Wool." The problem was that most of the company's underwear had as little as 10

percent wool and some contained no wool at all. The FTC issued a cease and desist order against Winsted for deceptive
practices and the Supreme Court of the United States upheld
the FTC ruling. Justice Brandeis, speaking for the Court, said:
"When misbranded goods attract customers by means of fraud
which they [the manufacturers or sellers] perpetrate, trade is
diverted from the producer of truthfully marked goods" (*FTC
v. Winsted Hosiery Co.*, 42 S. Ct. 384). In effect, the Court's
decision gave the FTC some real teeth. It meant that the FTC
could now move against deceptive practices with good, solid
legal support. A number of cases followed, but we are especially
interested in what happened in the visual field, for this is what
concerns the photographer.

Television: This is the area that has been one of the prime
targets for the FTC. It should be noted that the law in this
area has taken many different twists and turns, but at each
such twist and turn a new route opens up. For example, in
1963 a shaving cream company used television to show how
their shaving cream stayed moist while some of the others dried
out. The crux of this case was that ordinary lather shown on
the television screen wasn't lather at all, but a mock-up* made
from water and a foaming agent. Apparently, this mock-up did
not contain certain of the necessary ingredients which are used
to prevent shaving creams from drying up. Actually, the com-
peting brands did not dry out any more than the maker's did.
The FTC stepped in and said that the demonstration was false
because it misled and deceived the public. The FTC ordered
the maker to cease and desist.

The maker appealed and the appeals court looked at the decision a bit differently. The opening statement by the judge,
ironically, named Judge Wisdom, is particularly enlightening:

> Everyone knows that on TV all that glitters is not gold. On a
> black and white screen, white looks gray and blue looks
> white: the lily must be painted. Coffee looks like mud. Real
> ice cream melts much more quickly than that firm but fake
> sundae. The plain fact is, except by props and mock-ups,
> some objects cannot be shown on television as the viewer, in
> his mind's eye, knows the essence of the objects. (*Carter
> Products* v. *FTC*, 323 F2d 523)

---

*A mock-up is a kind of prop when the real thing is not available or is not being
used.

At the time the FTC had issued its decision in the above matter, it was of the opinion that mock-ups could not be used; that actual products had to be used in advertisements. But, with the Wisdom decision, that interpretation was redrawn on the basis that props and mock-ups could be used in a demonstration which was fair to the viewer in terms of the qualities of the products being simulated. What we then have is the inevitable: the collision between truth and salesmanship.

In 1965, the Court leaped into the fray regarding mock-ups (*Libbey-Owens-Ford Glass Co.* v. *FTC*, 352 F2d 415). The FTC had found that certain television commercials of a glass manufacturer and an automobile manufacturer contained false representations by stating that the automobile manufacturer's cars used plate glass but that another manufacturer used sheet glass. Whether it was true or not, the problem was that the commercials apparently contained false demonstrations achieved by the use of undisclosed mock-ups.

The commercials attempted to exaggerate the distortion in the sheet glass by applying vaseline to it, thereby showing the glass as being streaky. To show the superiority of the plate glass, a scene was shot through an open window. The court had a field day. It said that the undisclosed use of mock-ups was a deceptive practice notwithstanding the fact that the particular demonstration actually proved the product claim.

This happened too in the famous sandpaper test, known as the "Great Sandpaper Shave Case" (*FTC* v. *Colgate-Palmolive*, 85 S. Ct. 1035 (1965)). A shaving cream manufacturer put two well-known athletes in front of the television camera to show how their shaving cream could take care of the sandpaper beards of the two football players. To emphasize the point, the commercial showed the shaving of what appeared to be sandpaper.

The Court found the commercial deceptive in that the particular brand of shaving cream could not shave real sandpaper even after an hour's soaking. The Court said that the fact that no one buys shaving cream to scrape sandpaper was beside the point, for even if the commercial truthfully described the shaving cream's effectiveness, it was still deceptive and unfair advertising because it misinformed the viewer that what he saw being shaved was genuine, dry sandpaper. Oh, didn't we tell you? The manufacturer didn't really use sandpaper. He used plexiglass with sand glued to it.

Like anything else, the demarcation lines continue to get grayer. The customer is entitled to get what he is led to believe he will get. It should be recognized that if the only untruth is that what the viewer sees is artificial, yet the visual appearance is otherwise a correct representation of the product itself, then there is no deception. Remember, the viewer is not really buying the specific object under the studio lights; he is buying the product. Accordingly, it should be exactly as he understood it would be.

In the print area, the law says that if an advertisement contains a false claim inducing the purchase of a product inferior to the product the consumer expects to receive, then there is material deceit. This occurred recently when a soup company, in order to show the vegetable quantity of their soup, placed marbles at the bottom of the bowl, thus pushing the vegetables to the top. The poor consumer thought there were more vegetables than there really were.

Things are beginning to change today in this field of false advertising. For example, when television manufacturers advertise their sets, you will see language stripped across the bottom of a picture saying "actual closed circuit picture" or "simulated picture." Even with television commercials, the manufacturers are wising up. Many a dramatic commercial will begin with the words "A Dramatization" stripped across the bottom of the screen. Okay, now, with all this under our belt, how does the photographer fit in? Where is his liability?

Let's take the two cases we cited at the beginning of this chapter. In the first, the photographer would not be liable for the taking of the photograph of the two encyclopedia "salesmen." Why? Because the proper criterion for deciding a question of liability is the extent to which the photographer participated in the deception. A mere agent is not to be held responsible for *unknowingly* (and that's the key word) carrying out the orders of his principal. So, if the photographer did not know who he was photographing, he should not be held responsible for the deception.

In view of that point, the answer is really quite simple in the second case. The photographer knew what he was doing. He participated in the fraud and he could not escape liability.

Following this concept a bit further: In the glass case, the glass manufacturer claimed that he should not be liable for the use of the particular mock-ups because the film producer was the one who utilized them. The manufacturer said that he directed its advertising agency to present a fair commercial and that he was not aware of the manipulations of the film producer.

The court in its decison ruled that the manufacturer could *not* delegate its advertising to an independent contractor in order to escape liability.

What about the film producer?

Again, we go back to the criterion established for the photographer. Did he knowingly carry out the orders of his principal?

What can the photographer do about all this? Basically, the procedure is no different from that which he established in photographing models. He must obtain a release or, if that is not possible, at least a commitment that if there is any claim against him because he is carrying out the instructions of his principal, he will be idemnified against liability.

It should be noted that manufacturers today are not sitting idly by waiting for more problems with the FTC, because when the public learns about them, it generally turns away from their product.

In 1973, as a result of extensive hearings into the advertising field, a staff report to the Federal Trade Commission by John A. Howard and James Hulbert (published by Crain Communications, Inc.) was issued, under the title "Advertising and the Public Interest."

It was noted that in the area of photographing certain products, the report said that according to the testimony of Ms. Peggy Kohl, assistant director, General Foods Kitchens, it was not always possible, because of technical reasons, to use certain foods in certain demonstrations. There were problems of studio lights, lack of proper equipment to keep foods fresh, etc.

As Ms. Kohl stated, even today, "every now and then there is a great tasting recipe which is downright ugly in an honest photograph." She says that General Foods avoids this problem by not photographing such foods. In fact, they even have a policy which says mock-ups cannot be used. Ms. Kohl adds that the intent here is to ensure that "consumers should be provided with correct visual impression(s) of the quality, attributes, and amount of product they will receive." The report goes on to state that "while this policy tends to eliminate less-photogenic foods, it does provide clear-cut rules for home economists and agency personnel to follow." The point here is that the General Foods policy shows it is possible to develop guidelines of protection. Their policy, in fact, is as set forth below:

GENERAL FOODS' POLICY FOR FOOD PHOTOGRAPHY

1. Food will be photographed in an unadulterated state—product must be typical of that normally packed with no preselection for quality or substitution of individual components.
2. Individual portions must conform to amount per serving used in describing yield.
3. Package amounts shown must conform to package yield.
4. Product must be prepared according to package directions.
5. Recipe must follow directions and be shown in same condition it would appear when suitable for serving.
6. Mock-ups may not be used.
7. Props should be typical of those readily available to the consumers.
8. Theatrical devices (camera angles, small-size bowls and spoons) may not be used to convey attributes other than those normally seen in use.

The photographer now must consider this kind of policy in his work, which may in the future be issued by more and more companies. Chances are, if it has not already happened, specific instructions and restrictions may wind up in the various assignment agreements and the photographer must be aware that violation of such a restriction could open him to liability.

TO SUMMARIZE

Generally, the photographer will not be held liable for deception if he did not know anything about it. But even then, the photographer must watch himself carefully. The photographer must learn to protect himself against any claims of fraud as a participant to deception.

If the subject matter to be photographed is clearly misleading in size, content or form, then beware!

12

Can I Use My Pictures in Other Media?

It was not too long ago that the photographer was limited in his field of activity. For the most part, he was a portrait photographer. Slowly, but surely, his work branched out into other areas: commercial and advertising photography, then into the news media, as a photojournalist, and in allied fields. In fact, many former still photographers have now taken up positions behind the lenses of motion picture cameras. They have become cinematographers. Some have even gone another step and now sit behind the camera in the director's chair.

This is not farfetched. The photographer of today has a wide choice of areas in which he can work. With some imagination and a realization of what is going on around him, the photographer's possibilities are almost unlimited. As we mentioned before, book publishing, for example, has leaped forward and as a result, offers extremely rewarding subsidiary rights.

Let's turn to some of those areas which have opened up for the photographer.

TELEVISION

Photography is being used as never before. As we indicated in our chapter on book publishing, the demand for film documentaries of picture books is growing. Advertisers are also using photography, as witness the beautiful commercials done by Kodak recently: a series of still shots, blending smoothly into the sponsor's message. We mentioned documentaries. It is not any big surprise to see entire programs produced, made up of individual shots woven together by solid narration. Even film work often is interspersed with particular still shots.

MOTION PICTURES

More and more stills are being used. Remember the montage scenes from "Butch Cassiday" and "Parallax View" to name only two?

PHONOGRAPH RECORDS

Little explanation is needed. Photography's use has increased for album covers, inserts, etc.

POSTCARDS, POSTERS, CALENDARS, ETC.

Prices being paid now are moving upwards and when the Post Office tells us it estimates it handles more than a billion picture postcards a year, that's nothing to sneeze about. Today, posters and calendars are utilizing photography in greater number. Look also at the greeting card companies. Photography is being used more frequently here too.

Did we mention advertising? One major department store in New York City last year decided to do away with the sketch ads and moved into photography. All of their ads (and they do quite a volume) had the merchandise displayed by photography —full pages, no less.

Outdoor photography is also in use. Billboards now feature the use of photography more than ever before. When was the last time you saw a cartoon character or a drawing of someone smoking a cigarette? It's all from the view of the camera.

Packaging is another new market. Photography is being utilized on more and more packaging materials. Boxes of shave lotion, bath oil, and other toiletries now feature shots of burly men, sexy women and skimobiles.

Merchandising is another outgrowth. T-shirts, pillows, sheets, towels are now starring photography.

How about filmstrips, audio-visual uses? More and more, especially in the educational field.

Corporate annual reports now describe the many functions of a company by showing those functions through the camera's eye. And, of course, the shareholders can now see what their executives look like. Pictures of the board chairman on up have become an integral part of that report.

THEATER, ART

The theater is beginning to utilize photography too. How? Rear-screen effects, special effects, etc. The stage has certainly broadened its horizon in presenting new and dramatic avenues to the public and photography has been a part of this new approach.

Photography is art and many people are finding it satisfying to have their homes adorned with photography rather than oils on canvas. Many photographers' works are now being shown in galleries and often such work is being sold on the same basis as paintings. Recently, some well-known works were sold in special auctions for thousands of dollars—just like paintings.

The fact is that photography is the medium of the future. Some say it was always meant to be that. Visual representation is still in the vanguard of the arts and as we detailed in our opening chapter, photography is climbing ever upward with new technological developments and procedures.

Education has picked up the banner, and extensive courses in almost every aspect of photography are being offered at various educational centers around the country.

Photography is truly emerging from the shadows. It is now part and parcel of our everyday life and its effect is being seen around the globe.

The changes will continue to occur and the photographer should and must recognize the various legal effects of each change that takes place in his field. It is in this way that he can learn to protect himself and he can do this only by making sure he is treating himself as the professional he really is.

TO SUMMARIZE

What it really comes down to is this: if you want dignity, re-

spect and compensation for what you do as a photographer, then
know your rights. If your rights are violated, then enforce them.
If you fail to do this—if you fail to protect yourself—if you fail
to think of yourself as a professional, then you will never attain
that dignity—and you will never receive that respect—and you
damn well won't be paid!

Table of Cases

Index

THE AUTHORS

ROBERT M. CAVALLO is an attorney specializing in photography law. He is counsel to the Society of Photographers in Communications (ASMP), an organization of over a thousand of the most prominent photographers in the world. Additionally, he represents ten of the major photographic agencies in New York City as well as a number of the leading photographers in the country.

Mr. Cavallo has been a guest lecturer at various communication centers throughout the United States and also teaches a course in photographic law at New York University.

STUART KAHAN's background includes a number of years in the contract and business affairs departments of the William Morris Theatrical Agency and Paramount Pictures Corporation. He has been involved in many of the important and precedent-setting arrangements in the television, motion picture and book publishing fields. Mr. Kahan is the author of numerous articles on the theatrical field and recently completed a first novel.